Dear Edith

A late birthday present for you

I hope you enjoy it.

With love , Cloud

+ with love from Gill

1995

Julie Andrews

Julie Andrews accepts an Academy Award for Best Actress for her role in the film *Mary Poppins*. (1965).

JULIE ANDREWS

A Bio-Bibliography

Les Spindle

Bio-Bibliographies in the Performing Arts, Number 6
James Robert Parish, Series Editor

GREENWOOD PRESS
New York • Westport, Connecticut • London

Library of Congress Cataloging-in-Publication Data

Spindle, Les.
  Julie Andrews : a bio-bibliography / Les Spindle.
    p. cm. — (Bio-bibliographies in the performing arts, ISSN
0892-5550 ; no. 6)
  Discography: p.
  Bibliography: p.
  Includes index.
  ISBN 0-313-26223-3 (lib. bdg. : alk. paper)
  1. Andrews, Julie. 2. Andrews, Julie—Bibliography. 3. Motion
picture actors and actresses—Great Britain—Biography. 4. Singers—
Great Britain—Biography. I. Title. II. Series.
PN2598.A65S65 1989
791.43'028'092—dc20   89-7509

British Library Cataloguing in Publication Data is available.

Library of Congress Catalog Card Number: 89-7509
ISBN: 0-313-26223-3
ISSN: 0892-5550

First published in 1989

Greenwood Press, Inc.
88 Post Road West, Westport, Connecticut 06881

Printed in the United States of America

The paper used in this book complies with the
Permanent Paper Standard issued by the National
Information Standards Organization (Z39.48-1984).

10 9 8 7 6 5 4 3 2 1

*This book is dedicated to my sister, Nancy,
and her husband, Robert,
who were tremendously supportive in the launching
and development of my writing career.*

Contents

Photo Essay Following Biography

Preface

The most remarkable thing about Julie Andrews' roller-coaster career as a movie actress is how she manages to remain such a famous and admired *celebrity* years after she ceased to be a Hollywood superstar.

Fifteen years after her boxoffice popularity had peaked, Julie triumphantly resurfaced as a bona-fide film star in *Victor/Victoria* (1982). Then four years later, she jettisoned any lingering doubts about her abilities as a first-rate dramatic actress with brilliant performances in *That's Life!* and *Duet For One*.

From *Mary Poppins* to *Duet For One* has not been an easy journey for Julie, who had to endure vicious media gossip, fickle Hollywood casting practices, a scarcity of good women's roles, and capricious public loyalty.

Consequently, Julie's body of work is incredibly small for a performer of her calibre -- 16 films, 3 Broadway shows, a short-lived TV series and occasional specials. It is ironic and highly regrettable that a multimedia star who is as talented, vivacious, and acclaimed as Julie should enjoy such an uncommonly short reign as Hollywood's top female boxoffice draw in the mid-60s. Julie ruled the Hollywood roost and was the most sought-after film star through only six films within a span of four short years (1964-1968).

Yet, history has a way of recognizing extraordinary talents, and Julie will surely go down as one of the best. It is to her great credit that she has continued to explore ways to expand and enrich her talents despite the way a fickle and callous Hollywood has treated her.

Moreover, she has held her head high in the face of intense criticism. She remains a dignified and graceful presence in an industry rampant with crass commercialism, mean-spirited trends in pop entertainment, unscrupulous professional ethics, and plain old low class. Julie has never suffered from a scarcity of either class or integrity.

The severest test that she faced was in withstanding a vicious, widespread media smear campaign that dogged her for years following the boxoffice failures of both *Star!* (1968) and *Darling Lili* (1970). In a manner that is all too typical in Hollywood, the same journalists who had put Julie on a pedestal when her early films were shattering worldwide boxoffice records suddenly hastened to jump on the *crucify-Julie* bandwagon when it became clear she was not infallible.

One could perhaps blame this sudden change in attitude on reports from the set of *Darling Lili*, Julie's first film with Blake Edwards, whom she married after the film was completed. Reports circulated of arrogance, tantrums, extreme extravagance, and pure prima donna stubbornness on the part of the director and his leading lady. But these reports, whether true or not, did not justify the ruthless, unprofessional series of seemingly endless attacks from print and broadcast journalists that followed. What ever happened to journalistic objectivity?

Although it was probably little comfort for Julie to realize it, this type of switch in media attitude was not unique to her. The same sort of harassment has plagued many other film stars over the years, suggesting that it is almost a Hollywood ritual. Build them up, then tear them down. One or two columnists decide to take a mean-spirited slant towards a particular successful celebrity, and the rest follow along like sheep.

Nonetheless, it would be an oversimplification to blame all of Julie's career problems on the media. The failure of Hollywood studio executives to come up with enough suitable properties for such a multitalented performer was clearly another factor. The shifting tastes of an unpredictable moviegoing public could also be cited. After supporting Julie through excellent films (*Mary Poppins, The Sound of Music*), good films (*Hawaii, Thoroughly Modern Millie*), and even a seriously flawed film (*Torn Curtain*), they suddenly pulled out their support, staying away from *Star!* and *Darling Lili* in droves.

As discussed in more detail in the Filmography section of this book (**F08, F09**), both of these films have grown in stature in recent years, suggesting that their failures were due more to misguided marketing and distribution campaigns than to serious artistic shortcomings.

Despite these troubles, Julie has retained a fiercely loyal following all over the world, as I discovered when researching this book. Fans as far away as Denmark and South America contacted me, eagerly volunteering data from their extensive collections.

If you watch one of Julie's occasional guest appearances on television, you may be surprised to note that she seems more glamorous and charming than ever before. (She's one of the lucky few who grow more beautiful as they get older.)

Although we have only had a few opportunities to see Julie in new films or television shows during the past two decades, the initial impact she made in her spectacular early efforts still provides enough impetus to keep her a familiar and admired personality to people of all ages. *The Sound of Music* remains one of the most popular videocassettes in both sales and rental statistics. More than two decades after her most commercially successful show business efforts, the magic is still there.

Besides determination and hard work, the key to Julie's incredible survival against fearsome odds has been sheer talent. A flawless singer (*My Fair Lady, Mary Poppins*), a skilled comedienne (*Thoroughly Modern Millie*), a superb dramatic actress (*Duet For One*), a sparkling personality (ABC-TV's *Julie Andrews Hour*), Julie has never ceased to amaze us with her versatility. The risks she has taken in continually striving to stretch her abilities are rare in Hollywood, which is more accustomed to developing plastic stars all shaped from the same mold.

Thanks to her good sense and good taste, she has consistently worked with top directors, writers, and production personnel in first-class productions. (Her television variety efforts, for example -- including both her 1972 series and her specials -- have garnered dozens of Emmy nominations and critical raves.) Unlike other stars whose careers have peaked, she has never resorted to low-budget potboilers or assembly-line studio movies merely to be seen on the screen.

She is very selective about the roles she will accept, and she has given professional-calibre performances even when working with scripts that left a lot to be desired (as in *Torn Curtain* and *The Man Who Loved Women*). She has never been willing to settle for second best.

As Professor Higgins himself might have put it, "By George, Eliza, you've done it!"

The Format of This Book

Not a typical fan magazine-styled biography, nor a trivia buff's collection of miscellaneous star data, this book is intended as a complete all-in-one reference to the highly distinguished career of Julie Andrews.

Combining a share of my own personal observations with as many pure facts as I was able to dig out, the book is intended to be a comprehensive and accurate profile of the people, projects, artistic highs and lows, and general influences that brought Julie into the mainstream public consciousness in the late 1950s and have kept her there ever since.

All of the major aspects of her career -- theatre, film, personal appearances, television, recordings, and even children's fiction -- are included here with as much detail as I was able to supply.

To start off the book, a brief biography and chronology are included to serve as a summary of the major events of her life. As for the behind-the-scenes details or the *National Enquirer* slant on her life, I will leave that for another writer. The purpose of the biographical data here is simply to round out the book with the important milestones of Julie's life.

After that, the next four chapters cover her major career achievements in detail, including Filmography, Stage Appearances (including theatre, concerts, and live personal appearances), Television Appearances, and Discography. All of the individual entries in each of these four sections correspond to a particular career achievement and are numbered consecutively for convenient use of the subject index and for cross referencing within the chapters. Career events in each section are listed chronologically, then numbered consecutively. Filmography entries begin with **F01**...etc., Stage Appearances with **S01**...etc., Television Appearances with **T01**...etc., and Discography entries with **D01**...etc.

For example, her first film *Mary Poppins* is assigned number **F01**, her eighteenth film, *Duet For One*, number **F18**. If you are reading about *Mary Poppins* in the Filmography section and you want to know what songs were included in the film, the *Poppins* synopsis tells you to turn to Discography entry number **D15**, where the *Mary Poppins* film soundtrack is detailed. The Television Appearances and Stage Appearances sections use the same method to refer to soundtracks and cast albums, listing musical numbers for the television shows and stage productions in the Discography section only.

Following the four career event chapters is a bibliography (with entries numbered **B01**,...etc.), listing more than 150 reference sources for more information on Julie, including books, and magazine and newspaper articles.

The appendices include a list of various show business awards that Julie has won or received nominations for, including Oscars, Tonys, Emmys, Grammys, Golden Globes, and others (Appendix A), a list of theatre and film projects Julie *almost* performed in (Appendix B), and descriptions of the two children's books that Julie has written (Appendix C).

The Subject Index includes page numbers and/or section entry numbers (such as **F01**) for reference. For each index entry, I have used whichever method appeared to be the quickest way for the reader to locate the listed topic. In some cases (usually for shorter entries), the section entry numbers were better. In other cases, the page numbers seemed more helpful.

Your suggestions for additions or corrections for future editions of this book are welcome, as are embellishments to any of the details that I have provided here. Send them to me in care of Greenwood Press, Westport, Connecticut.

Acknowledgments

I wish to express my heartfelt gratitude to the following individuals, who were extremely helpful in my research for this book: Carol Borsheim, Stephen Eberly, Sharon R. Fox, Alex Gildzen, Robert S. Jones, William Torbert Leonard, Robin Little (editor of *Films in Review*), Doug McClelland, Jim Meyer, the Movie/Entertainment Book Club, Elaine P. Murphy, Richard Pearson, Robert Rosterman, Michael R. Pitts, Vincent Terrace, Marie-Jeanne van Hovell, Bob Vaubel, Tom Wilson, and Anders Zakrisson.

I wish to express special thanks to Marilyn Brownstein and James Robert Parish, who gave the green light to this project and provided invaluable feedback as to its form and content.

Julie Andrews

Biography

Even as an infant, Julia Elizabeth Wells had the sound of music ringing in her ears. Her mother, Barbara Morris Wells, was a talented amateur pianist who could not afford a babysitter and was thus forced to take baby Julia along to her part-time job as a dance school accompanist.

Born October 1, 1935, in Walton-on-Thames, Surrey (a suburb of London), young Julie (as she came to be known) grew up around a show business environment. Her family, though impoverished, worked in various aspects of show business throughout Julia's childhood and teen years.

Julie's aunt, Joan Morris (Barbara's sister) was a dance instructor. She owned the dance school where Barbara served as rehearsal and performance accompanist. Barbara and Joan's father (Julie's grandfather) was an accomplished drum major in the British Grenadier Guards. Although Julie's real father, Edward C. (Ted) Wells was a teacher of woodworking, with no artistic talent other than an appreciation of poetry and literature, Julie was raised from age 5 by her stepfather, Edward (another Ted) Andrews, a vaudeville entertainer from Canada. Barbara Morris Wells became Barbara Morris Andrews in 1939, shortly after her divorce from Ted Wells. Julia's last name was legally changed to Andrews and she eventually altered the name *Julia* to *Julie*.

Although Ted Andrews was probably the strongest single influence in encouraging young Julie to pursue a show business career and introduced her to some important people, there had been earlier examples of Julie's career destiny.

In the years prior to Barbara's divorce and subsequent remarriage, Julie spent many of her waking hours at Joan Morris' dance school. Not only were her mother and aunt actively involved in the classes and student showcase performances, but her father Ted Wells was a valuable resource for set construction, due to his skill as a woodworker.

Since she was two, Julie took ballet and tap classes from Joan. She displayed a quick aptitude for dancing and playacting. The adults who came in contact with her were impressed with her vivid creative imagination.

At the age of 2 1/2, Julie was assigned a bit part as a fairy in one of Joan's performances. Two years later, Joan gave her a part that included song, dialogue, and dance, and she received an enthusiastic ovation for her performance.

The breakup of her parents' marriage was not an easy thing for four-year old Julie to endure. She was close to her real father, who spent a lot of time teaching her to read and write and to appreciate poetry and literature. Her parents had agreed not to send her to a regular school right away, which was quite a daring departure from convention at the time. They wanted to allow her to explore her talents to discover what areas of study would be best suited for her before she embarked on a formal education.

Julie's younger brother, John, was born in 1939, the same year that Barbara met Ted Andrews. Barbara had signed up for a summer season of work as a pianist for the variety show, *Dazzle Company*, in Bognor Regis. Andrews was billed in the show as *The Canadian Troubadour: Songs and a Guitar*. A quick friendship developed between Barbara Wells and Ted Andrews.

When World War II erupted in Europe in September of that year, the *Dazzle Company* broke up. Both Barbara Wells and Ted Andrews joined ENSA, the volunteer organization that entertained the British troops. By now, it was evident that a romance between the two had developed. The marriage between Barbara and Ted Wells collapsed, and shortly afterwards, Barbara became Mrs. Ted Andrews.

Ted Wells had been given custody of both Julie and John, but voluntarily allowed Julie's mother and new stepfather to raise her. Although Wells and Julie had a very close relationship, Wells decided that Julie would have the best chance of launching a professional career as a performer living with Barbara and Ted Andrews.

Julie went to live with the Andrews, who had moved to London. She reluctantly left all of her childhood friends from Walton-on-Thames behind, as well as her father and baby brother. Although the collapse of the family appeared to be more amicable than most (especially considering the circumstances that caused it), this series of events was to take its emotional toll on Julie in the years to come. Perhaps viewing Ted Andrews as the catalyst who had instigated the family breakup, Julie did not approach her new stepfather with a positive first impression.

Ted Wells shortly thereafter married a hairdresser, Win. They had a daughter of their own, Celia. Julie acquired two stepbrothers when Donald and Chris were born to her mother and stepfather.

In the first few years of the Andrews marriage, the family had a difficult time making ends meet, but the situation improved considerably when Barbara and Ted Andrews began to develop a solid reputation as a strong second act on vaudeville bills. In 1943, this enabled the family to move from the seedier portions of London to a nicer home in Beckenham, Kent.

The Andrews occasionally joined their neighbors in air raid shelters whenever German bomber planes appeared to be approaching the area. This was, of course, a terrifying time for all. In an effort to get through the ordeal, the crowd would sometimes join Ted Andrews in an *a cappela* chorus. Julie's voice drew attention when she unwittingly sang an octave above the crowd's.

Becoming more aware of Julie's freak voice, Ted decided to enlist a vocal instructor to develop it. Madame Lilian Stiles-Allen was an excellent concert singer who worked hard to help Julie hone her natural abilities. She remained an important influence on Julie's professional and personal development for many years to come.

Despite her dislike of Ted Andrews in the early years, it was to become clear to Julie later on that he clearly had wanted the best for her. He was a strict disciplinarian when she was in training, and saw to it that she religiously accomplished her daily practice sessions.

He decided to enroll her in a performing arts school in London, where she studied acting and ballet, as well as general academic subjects. During this time, she spent a large share of her time under the supervision of the family housekeeper, as her parents were frequently on tour. She would usually be reunited with them during school holidays, travelling to wherever they happened to be performing at the time.

In 1946, after the war had ended, the family decided to move back to Julie's birthplace, Walton-on-Thames. Soon thereafter, Julie made her first public singing appearance in her parents' vaudeville act. She was allowed to do this occasionally during the next few years.

A big break came in Fall, 1947, when Ted introduced Julie to Val Parnell of the well known theatrical booking firm, Moss Empires. Parnell booked talent for most of the major theatres in the London area, including the Hippodrome and the London Palladium.

Parnell signed Julie on the spot for her first professional stage appearance without her parents. She made her debut in the *Starlight Roof* revue at the Hippodrome. She sang a song that she had perfected through hours of practice, the challenging "I Am Titania" aria from the opera *Mignon*. The audience response was jubilant, and Julie walked away with better reviews than anyone else in the company. Several important career opportunities resulted from her performance in the revue.

She was introduced to Charles Tucker during the run of the show. He was a theatrical manager who was to serve Julie for the next 20 years, providing valuable advice and solid career opportunities.

Starlight Roof also led to Julie's first screen test. She auditioned for Joe Pasternak, an American producer specializing in film musicals, at the London headquarters of Metro-Goldwyn-Mayer. He apparently was not sufficiently impressed to give Julie an opportunity at that point.

A more successful result of the revue was Julie's subsequent request to appear in a Royal Command Performance at the London Palladium, which toplined Danny Kaye. The performance, on November 1, 1948, was played to an impressive audience, most notably Queen Elizabeth and Princess Margaret. The Queen made a special point of staying to greet Julie after the performance to congratulate her.

In 1948, when Julie was 15, she first met Tony Walton (her future husband), who was 14. She was appearing in *Humpty Dumpty* at the London Casino, and Tony and his brother Richard were in the audience. He and Julie conversed on the train back to Walton-on-Thames, as he lived nearby. The two of them began corresponding and visiting each other whenever possible. They developed a close friendship that was to endure as they grew to adulthood, blossoming into romance, and eventually marriage.

In 1950, Julie began performing regularly on the British Broadcasting Company's radio comedy series, *Educating Archie*. She achieved fame throughout England for her work on the show, which she continued until 1952, when she left the cast.

Several concert appearances occupied her time during this period, including a 1949 engagement with her parents at the Coconut Grove and the Hippodrome in Blackpool, a 1950 engagement at the Winter Garden in Margate, and 1951 appearances in Yorkshire and Manchester.

Julie was also enjoying her success in pantomime productions, which included *Little Red Riding Hood* at Nottingham (Christmas, 1950) and *Jack and the Beanstalk* at Coventry (Christmas, 1952). She seemed quite content with the *status quo* state of her career for the time being, and was not really prepared for the abrupt change that was facing her when a surprise visitor came to see her after a 1953 performance of *Cinderella* at the London Palladium.

She was greeted backstage by Vida Hope, the director of the hit London musical, *The Boy Friend*. To Julie's great surprise, Hope informed her that *The Boy Friend* was preparing a Broadway opening, and the producers wanted Julie to play the female lead role of Polly Browne. This was clearly the chance of a lifetime that hundreds of young actresses would have died for.

However, Julie was not anxious to leave her family and friends for two years. Somewhat stunned by the sudden offer, feeling fearful and unsure, Julie surprised Hope by answering with a sudden but quite firm "No."

Her friends and family and her agent, Charlie Tucker, were flabbergasted when Julie told them what she had done. They badgered her mercilessly to reconsider, but she steadfastly stuck to her decision. During the two decades that Charlie Tucker managed her career, this was one of the few times that Julie went against his advice.

The issue appeared to be over when Julie accepted a role in a new play going on tour for an open-ended run, eventually to open in London. The play was an American drama with music called *Mountain Fire*, written by Howard Richardson and William Bearney. Quite a departure for Julie, the play called for her to play a Southern belle who became pregnant out of wedlock. The play opened in March, 1954 in Liverpool, next moving to Leeds and Birmingham.

During the run of the show, Julie fell in love with one of her costars, Neil McCallum, a Canadian. This caused problems for her already shaky romance with Tony Walton, who was very much in love with her.

Her serenity in not having to face the *Boy Friend* dilemma came to an abrupt halt one night, when Vida Hope attended a performance of *Mountain Fire* with Cy Feurer, who was set to direct the U.S. production of *The Boy Friend.* They visited Julie after the show and again brought up the proposition of her Broadway debut.

This time, she couldn't bring herself to give a direct no, and left the issue open-ended. Once again, her family and friends pleaded with her not to pass up what was sure to be a rare career opportunity.

Julie was wavering, but there were complications. Besides her growing infatuation for Neil MacCallum, Julie was also concerned about the problems her mother and stepfather were having. Their marriage had become rather tumultuous, Ted Andrews had taken to nasty drinking bouts, and it began to look like a second divorce for Barbara might be in the offing.

For these reasons, it was all the more difficult for Julie to consider leaving England for two years. However, something occurred that appeared to resolve her dilemma. *Mountain Fire* never made it on its destination to London, closing while still on tour. The play received disastrous reviews and shut down in August, 1954. This occurrence, coupled with the persistent pleadings of Charlie Tucker, finally prompted Julie to give in. However, she insisted that, unlike the rest of the cast, her contract would not exceed one year. The producers agreed, paving the way for Julie to go to Broadway.

In August, 1954, just before she was to leave for New York, Julie had a bitter fight with Tony Walton, who was hurt at having been brushed aside for another young man. As Julie left for the U.S., it appeared doubtful that they would continue corresponding or remain friends.

That same month, the problems between Ted and Barbara Andrews intensified, resulting in Barbara taking out a restraining order to keep Ted away from her. A month later, they separated amidst an ugly courtroom scene, with each side claiming ownership of the family house. The judge ruled in favor of Barbara.

Now on the threshold of adulthood, Julie was forced to follow her own destiny and hope that her friends and family could work out their problems without her. On August 23, 1954, she boarded the plane for her first trip to America, a trip destined to launch her into a career as an international superstar.

She travelled on the plane with another member of the *Boy Friend* cast, Dilys Laye (whom many critics were to compare fondly to Beatrice Lillie), and they developed an instant friendship. When they arrived in New York, they took an inexpensive room together at the Times Square Hotel.

On her first night in New York, Julie had her first taste of the glamorous Manhattan night life. She attended a party for the *Boy Friend* cast given by the show's producers, Cy Feurer (who was also directing the show) and Ernest Martin. The party was held at Sardi's Restaurant, the famous celebrity hangout where Broadway actors, actresses, and various theatre personnel frequently gathered after a performance.

The next five weeks were rigorous and exhausting for Julie. She was paid $100 a week, not a large salary for a Broadway lead actress even in the early 50s. After an intensive day of rehearsal, she would return to her hotel room to rest up for the next day's work. She and Dilys had moved into a modest apartment on Fifth Avenue.

Even more exhausting than the rigorous dancing and physical comedy required by the show, some very difficult behind-the-scenes tensions made *The Boy Friend* a particularly demanding experience for Julie. She was receiving an immediate introduction to the ups and downs of the competitive, high-strung world of the Broadway theatre.

As the show progressed towards its late September scheduled opening, major artistic differences surfaced, with Vida Hope and the show's author/composer Sandy Wilson on one side, and producers Feurer and Martin on the other. The producers insisted on altering the tone of the show, stepping up its pace to achieve their estimation of what Broadway audiences expected. Hope and Wilson vehemently protested, resulting in frequent clashes between the two sides. This ultimately led to the barring of Wilson and Hope from the theatre, with Feurer and Martin taking complete artistic control.

Though the show was shaping up nicely, Julie was unnerved by the unpleasant environment brought on by the dissensions. She approached opening night her usual fears and self-doubts (at least, usual at this phase of her career). A tremendous amount was at a stake for her, and she was understandably nervous about the outcome.

On September 30, 1954 (the night before Julie's nineteenth birthday), the show opened to a capacity audience, who reacted warmly and enthusiastically from the very outset. Julie's fears were instantly allayed. The entire performance was excellently received.

After the performance, Julie went out on the town with Bill Bearney, one of the *Mountain Fire* authors, who had become a good friend. They were celebrating a double occasion: the play opening and Julie's birthday at 12:00 midnight.

The light souffle of a show was highly praised by even the most hardboiled New York critics. Julie was singled out in almost every review. The job that she had so reluctantly accepted was now clearly a major milestone in her career.

Soon thereafter, Julie and her roommate moved to a penthouse on Park Avenue. She was beginning to warm up to America, and the intoxicating excitement of New York. But she also missed her friends and family tremendously and was looking forward to the end of her one-year contract.

On the heels of the successful *Boy Friend* opening, Julie received dozens of offers for TV and radio appearances and commercials. She accepted some of them out of a sense of obligation, but was not really comfortable with the star routine. She still yearned for the slower pace and less pressured show business environment of her homeland.

Her romantic life during that first year in the U.S. was unspectacular. She occasionally dated Bill Bearney, but essentially on a platonic level. For a while, she remained infatuated with Neil MacCallum, who had returned to Canada, but corresponded with Judy and even flew in to New York to see her once in a while. However, the spark of attraction between the two of them gradually diminished and before long they lost contact altogether. Julie made the first move in re-establishing correspondence with Tony Walton, and their friendship was soon regenerated with frequent letters back and forth.

Less than a month before Julie's scheduled return to England, her next big career break came when an agent of the famed composer/lyricist team Alan Jay Lerner/Frederick Loewe (*Brigadoon, Paint Your Wagon*) called to invite Julie to audition for them. The show was *My Fair Lady*, their upcoming musical based on George Bernard Shaw's classic comedy *Pygmalion*.

Julie auditioned for Lerner and Loewe and was awaiting their reaction, when she got another impressive call. This was to audition for another stellar Broadway composer, Richard Rodgers, for his upcoming musical, *Pipe Dream*. Together with his partner, Oscar Hammerstein II, he was a favorite of Julie's ever since she saw *South Pacific* in London as a young girl. He didn't hire Julie but was obviously impressed with her, as she later toplined two of his musicals created with Hammerstein (the television production of *Cinderella* in 1956 and the film version of *The Sound of Music* in 1965).

Shortly thereafter, Julie was called back to see Lerner and Loewe for a second audition. After the audition, she was offered the starring female lead role of Eliza Doolittle in *My Fair Lady*, opposite Rex Harrison. By now she was more career-driven, than she had been when she had almost lost *The Boy Friend* due to hesitation. This time, she instantly accepted the offer.

Her trip back to England would be for a shorter term than she had expected, but she would at least be with family and friends during the holidays. On October 1, 1955, Julie flew back home for the reunion with her family that she had been longing for during the entire year. (Curiously, her birthday continually seemed to coincide with new milestones in her life.)

Unfortunately, her time back home was once again cut shorter than expected by career demands. She had scarcely been home for a month when Charlie Tucker called her about another job offer.

He had arranged for Julie to costar with Bing Crosby in a major American network television special. It was a musical adaptation of Maxwell Anderson's fanciful play, *High Tor*. Julie would have to return to the U.S. immediately to begin rehearsals in Hollywood.

This dismayed Julie at first, because she had looked forward to this family vacation for so long. She would, however, be able to make it back home in time for a family Christmas celebration. She accepted the offer.

She enjoyed working with Bing Crosby and had a few new songs by Arthur Schwartz to sing. She was developing into a solidly professional actress and was becoming less concerned about her immediate wants and more concerned about what was best for her career. After working in Hollywood for two weeks, she returned home to celebrate the holidays. *High Tor* was scheduled for airing on the CBS network a few months later, in March, 1956, just a few days prior to the opening of *My Fair Lady*. When the show aired, it received a mixed critical reaction, but it was a good showcase for Julie and gave her maximum exposure throughout the U.S. as a new talent who audiences were sure to hear about again.

On January 1, 1956, Julie was back on the plane to New York to begin rehearsals with director Moss Hart and the cast of *My Fair Lady*. The show, of course, was the biggest challenge that Julie had faced up to that time. In the early rehearsals, she did not easily project all of the nuances of Eliza's character, nor could she convincingly convey Eliza's complete transformation from Cockney flower girl to aristocratic lady. This was perfectly understandable considering the limitation of her past acting experience, but it was nonetheless a problem when one considers *My Fair Lady's* distinguished cast of seasoned veterans, who could develop a solid characterization with very little rehearsal. Furthermore, this was one of the most anticipated musicals in years, and could not afford to be anything except first rate in every department. Julie found herself over her head and in deep trouble.

With Julie's job in jeopardy and precious little time left to look for a new Eliza, Moss Hart, in what is now a legendary move, took her in tow for a full weekend of drilling and coaching. He went over every line of the play with her and worked determinedly to help her find the core of Eliza's character and enough technique to project that character. The intense sessions apparently paid off, because Julie had improved 100% by Monday morning's rehearsal. Within a few days, she was projecting her character with the best of them and was no longer a liability to the production.

Julie fulfilled a long-time wish by paying to fly her mother out to share in her joyful experience. Barbara Andrews arrived a few days before the March 15 opening. Everything pointed to an impending blockbuster success, but Julie had now been around show business long enough to know that nothing could be taken for granted. This show wouldn't be over until the slender lady sang. She was quite nervous the last few days before opening, and understandably so. This was obviously the role that could push her to the top of full-fledged stardom...or just as easily sink her if she didn't come across. The stakes were frighteningly, unbelievably high.

Thankfully, as everyone had expected, Julie and the entire production passed the test with flying colors. It was a beautifully received performance on the part of audiences and critics alike. It was, in short, one of the most phenomenally triumphant premieres in the history of American theatre. There was no longer any doubt: a major superstar had arrived.

A month into the run, Julie was pleasantly surprised that Tony Walton was journeying to America to see her. They had completely patched up their estranged friendship during Julie's Christmas visit, and their differences appeared to be entirely behind them. Tony began accepting freelance job assignments doing art for magazines. His intended brief stay lingered on, and his relationship with Julie began to deepen.

During this period, Julie unquestionably was the toast of New York. She was recognized everywhere she went and her name became a staple in the gossip columns, a sure sign that you've made it in the Big Apple.

Her next important career opportunity came from Rodgers and Hammerstein, her favorite Broadway musical creators. It was not *The Sound of Music*, which was not to come her way for another decade. It was *Cinderella*, an original musical for television, the only such effort ever created by Rodgers and Hammerstein.

Julie worked on this show while still performing in *My Fair Lady*. She was already an important enough star that the producers of the *Cinderella* special were willing to set up their production schedule to accommodate her availability. The fact that Julie was able to juggle two such demanding projects at once and shine in both of them was a testament to her consummate professionalism, which by now was evident to everyone working with her.

Although the reviews for the broadcast itself (March 31, 1957) were not all enthusiastic, Julie came out smelling like a rose, as usual. It was beginning to look like she could do no wrong, which was the way her career was to continue for the next several years.

Celebrating her twenty-first birthday on October 1, 1956, Julie had matured immensely during those three years in the U.S. when she played in *The Boy Friend* and *My Fair Lady*. Though always close to her family, she had learned a greater sense of independence and self-confidence. The gawky little girl with the freak voice had blossomed into an internationally known television and stage celebrity, admired by fans and highly respected among her colleagues for her wit, intelligence, and extraordinary talent.

As Julie's contract for *My Fair Lady* was getting close to completion, she was looking forward to taking a well deserved two months off before reporting to the Drury Lane Theatre in London in April, 1958. She had contracted for another year of *My Fair Lady*, which was to have its English premiere with all of the principal Broadway players intact, including Rex Harrison and Stanley Holloway. Meanwhile, Sally Ann Howes was to replace Julie in the Broadway production.

In February, 1958, Julie left the show and flew to Paris for a vacation with her mother and Charlie Tucker. Several family members met them there, including her father, Ted Wells. After this visit, she flew alone to Switzerland, where she was joined by Tony Walton, on holiday from his Broadway job assignments. After this, she flew to London and settled into a luxurious suite at the Savoy Hotel, which was to be her home during the London run of the show.

My Fair Lady had its British premiere on April 30, 1958. It met with a reception equal to the jubilant Broadway response. Again, audiences and critics alike fell in love with the show and made it a record-breaking hit.

On May 10, 1959, Julie and Tony Walton finally confirmed the gossip column speculations by getting married at St. Mary's Church in Outlander, Waybridge. It was a lavish ceremony, with all of Julie and Tony's friends and family in attendance, including Ted and Barbara Andrews, who had reunited and were trying to make a go of their troubled marriage.

Julie had taken a brief hiatus from the show. The couple honeymooned in Los Angeles for a couple of weeks, then flew back to London, so Julie could return to the show.

In August, 1959, Julie left the cast of *My Fair Lady* with understandably mixed emotions. She had enjoyed the glorious success and the glamour that had been around the show since the beginning, but she was also tired, and wanted to take a break, then plunge into a new career challenge.

Offers for work in films, television, and stage had started pouring in shortly before the end of her London engagement. She wisely turned down an offer to take a small part in another George Bernard Shaw vehicle, a film version of his play *The Devil's Disciple*, starring Kirk Douglas and Burt Lancaster. Due to the size of the part, it would not have been the best career move at that point. Her screen debut deserved to be something more spectacular. She was hoping to be offered the chance to recreate her Eliza Doolittle role in Warner Brothers' big-budget film of *My Fair Lady*, and the buzz in show business circles was that she had the part in the bag.

Meanwhile, Julie began discussions with Lerner and Loewe about their next project, which was to be a lavish musical about the King Arthur legend, *Jenny Kissed Me*, based on T. H. White's book, *The Once and Future King*. Richard Burton had signed to make his Broadway singing debut in the role of King Arthur, and Julie was being courted to costar as his leading lady, Queen Guenevere.

Since she was at another major crossroad in her career, Julie did not make an immediate commitment, preferring to mull it over while she spent some precious time with her new husband. Now the situation was reverse, however. Tony's career was taking off in leaps and bounds. He was on the road a lot, flying between New York and London. Ironically, now that Julie was able to take a break, Tony's schedule did not allow them the time together that she had been looking forward to. From the outset, it was difficult for them to build a solid marriage, because their separate career demands seemed to be keeping them apart.

In February, 1960, Julie made the commitment to return to Broadway in the new Lerner/Loewe musical, now titled *Camelot* after its magical setting in the legendary days of King Arthur and his Knights of the Round Table. Julie would have several beautiful new songs to sing, a glamorous wardrobe, and a challenging dramatic role, giving her a chance to flex her acting muscles further. She signed to appear in the show for the first 18 months of its Broadway run, beginning in November of that year.

In August, Julie returned to New York to begin *Camelot* rehearsals, accompanied by Tony, who was designing the sets for Sandy Wilson's new musical, *Valmouth*. Pre-Broadway tryouts for *Camelot* began in Toronto, Canada in October. Since the show boasted many of the same creative talents as *My Fair Lady* (Julie, Lerner and Loewe, Moss Hart, and others), critics were quick to point out that this was not a fortunate comparison. *Camelot's* book lacked the polish and wit of *My Fair Lady's*. Unlike *My Fair Lady*, *Camelot* was not based on a literary masterpiece, and it was simply not in the same league. Comparisons were unfair, but probably unavoidable. The show was spectacularly mounted and showed tremendous promise, but still obviously needed a lot of play doctoring if it was to be the Broadway blockbuster that everyone had hoped for.

During subsequent tryout engagements, the show's creators worked hard to perfect their flawed gem. Further complications developed when Lerner was hospitalized with an ulcer flareup, soon followed by a heart attack for Moss Hart. The Broadway opening had to be postponed for two weeks, as Lerner had to take over the direction from Hart, who was not able to return to work. The show was revamped continually right up to opening night. It finally opened on December 3 to a record-breaking $3 million advance sale.

Although the show had improved tremendously from the early tryouts, it received a mixed critical reaction in New York. The production was opulent, stylish, and brilliantly acted, but many critics complained that the story was ponderous, the music unspectacular, and the show lacked dramatic impact.

As usual, Julie gathered pristine reviews, as did her costar, Richard Burton. Despite the disappointing reviews, the show clearly had enough star power and spectacle to shape up as a boxoffice success.

During the *Camelot* run, Julie and Tony's marriage reached its point of greatest harmony. Not only were they working close to one another and able to spend more time together, but each was highly successful in his/her respective career. Tony was designing the costumes for one of his biggest hits, *A Funny Thing Happened on the Way to the Forum*, starring Zero Mostel. In March 1962, it was announced that the Waltons were expecting their first child in November. The timing was fortunate, as Julie's run in *Camelot* was coming to an end.

In September 1962, Warner Bros. Pictures announced that Audrey Hepburn, not Julie Andrews, would costar with Rex Harrison in the plum role of Eliza Doolittle when *My Fair Lady* reached the motion picture screen. Though Julie has repeatedly tried to downplay her disappointment at this announcement over the years, it was the first real career slap-in-the-face she had received up to that point. Prior to this, her career had seemed like a fairy tale with a perpetual happy ending.

While Hollywood had frequently bypassed celebrated Broadway stars when transferring their star Broadway vehicles to film, this time the move came as a genuine shock to film industry watchers. Somehow, it seemed logical that Julie was destined for a screen career, and her association with this role was so strong that many had simply assumed there was no casting decision to be made. Julie was the shoo-in choice.

Jack L. Warner of Warner Bros. Pictures apparently felt differently. Aside from Robert Preston's role in *The Music Man*, Warners seemed very consistent in recasting Broadway star roles, i.e., Rosalind Russell for Ethel Merman in *Gypsy* (1962) and Lucille Ball for Angela Lansbury in *Mame* (1974). *My Fair Lady* was a multimillion dollar undertaking, one of the most anticipated films of the 60s. Warner obviously felt that casting a proven boxoffice name over a movie newcomer was the way to go.

This temporary dark cloud didn't last long, however. Julie's next major career break was germinating in the mind of another legendary show business figure who was smart enough to see her potential and propose a collaboration between the two of them. The smart man was Walt Disney, and the collaboration he had in mind was to star Julie in a project that was geared to be the crowning achievement of his career. He had seen Julie in *Camelot* on Broadway, and decided she would be perfect for the upcoming film that his studio was producing. Nothing short of perfection would do for the film -- or for its magical title character. *Mary Poppins* was the spectacular musical fantasy that Disney was so carefully nurturing, based on the series of children's books by Pamela (P.L.) Travers.

Just as she had done prior to her first big career breakthrough in *The Boy Friend*, Julie was not certain at first that *Poppins* would be a good career move. She did not say yes to Disney right away.

However, Disney was determined to win her over, and sweetened the pot by offering Tony Walton a plum assignment as set designer for the film. This project, a sugar-coated fantasy set in Edwardian England, was clearly a designer's dream. Besides, the exposure for Tony, who had previously worked primarily on stage design, would be invaluable. On top of all this, Julie and Tony could continue to see more of each other, which had helped to solidify their relationship during the run of *Camelot*. So Julie accepted.

Between Julie's stage triumphs and her upcoming film debut, she conquered another American medium, television. In June, 1962, she taped a special for CBS-TV, *Julie and Carol at Carnegie Hall*. She costarred with her good friend Carol Burnett in the hour of song, dance, and comedy sketches. She had first worked with Carol when she guested on CBS-TV's *The Garry Moore Show* in Spring, 1961, and the two musical comedy stars hit it off instantly, both personally and professionally. Their "Big D" production number from Frank Loesser's musical *Most Happy Fella* was a showstopper.

The *Julie and Carol* special was taped before a live audience at New York's Carnegie Hall in Spring 1962, for broadcast that June. Written by Mike Nichols and produced by Carol's husband at the time, Joe Hamilton, the show was filled with showstopping moments. Julie let her hair down to do some of her most boisterous clowning. The genuine friendship of the two stars shone threw, adding a special glow of warmth to the show.

Though it received mixed reactions from the critics when it first aired, the show later received an Emmy award as Best Musical Program, as well as the Rose D-O'r from the Montreaux International Film Festival.

Before *Mary Poppins* was to begin filming at the Disney studio near Hollywood in Spring 1963, Tony and Julie returned to England in September of the previous year to enjoy a rest and await the birth of their child. Emma Kate Walton was born on November 27, 1962 in London.

In January 1963, Tony returned to the U.S. to begin planning his designs for *Mary Poppins*. A few weeks later, Julie and her new baby daughter joined Tony in a house he had obtained for the family close to the Disney Studio. (Coincidentally, *My Fair Lady* was filming at Warner's Burbank studio, right next to the Disney lot.)

Julie relished the role of the practically perfect magical nanny, Mary Poppins. Unlike the awkward days when she struggled to keep up with the veteran *My Fair Lady* cast on Broadway, Julie was now an experienced actress -- letter-perfect in her dialogue, fastidious in her diction, and uncommonly sincere and believable before the cameras.

She got along well with her talented costar, Dick Van Dyke. The film was a labor of love on the part of everyone. Like *My Fair Lady*, it was that rare show business phenomenon that occurs when the right people get together at the right time with the right material. Everything was in perfect harmony.

From the earliest rushes, it was clear that Disney had something very special with his new leading lady and his spectacular musical film. The word around Hollywood was that Jack L. Warner had made a gigantic *faux pas* and that Walt Disney was the fortunate beneficiary of Warners' oversight.

Even before *Poppins* was finished filming, Julie was receiving offers to do more films. She committed to two. First up was her first nonmusical film, *The Americanization of Emily*, for MGM. This World War II comedy-drama, to costar James Garner, was a cynical and witty antiwar satire written by Paddy Chayefsky.

The other film was *The Sound of Music*, 20th Century-Fox's version of Rodgers and Hammerstein's last Broadway musical before Hammerstein's death. Mary Martin had created the role of Maria Von Trapp onstage, but she had never caught on as a film star, and was not seriously considered for the film. Doris Day and other actresses had been mentioned, but one look at Disney's advance footage of *Mary Poppins* convinced Robert Wise (who was to direct *The Sound of Music*) that Julie was his Maria.

In Summer 1963, the Waltons returned to London. Julie happily settled in as a doting mother and housewife for a few short months before returning to Hollywood for her film commitments. She had enjoyed a very satisfying professional experience with *Mary Poppins*, but was now ready for a little domesticity. Tony worked on the London edition of the Broadway musical, *A Funny Thing Happened on the Way to the Forum*, while Julie enjoyed her time off.

In late 1963, Julie returned to Hollywood to begin filming *The Americanization of Emily* on the MGM Studio lot. This was a challenging role for Julie, including both comic and dramatic scenes and her first screen lovemaking, opposite James Garner.

As Robert Wise had done, *Emily's* producer Martin Ransohoff had hired Julie on the basis of the *Mary Poppins* footage that he had seen. Unlike others in Hollywood, he obviously had not viewed Julie as a stereotypical goody-goody ingenue type, and gave her the type of well-rounded role that would be tougher and tougher for her to come by once she became imprisoned in a *Mary Poppins/Sound of Music* image.

It was during the filming of *Emily* that Julie first met Blake Edwards (her future husband) at a wrapup party after completion of his Peter Sellers film *A Shot in the Dark*. Edwards had established himself as a respected film director, due to the success of *The Pink Panther, Days of Wine and Roses*, and *Breakfast at Tiffany's*. Their meeting was casual and brief. Their paths were to cross many more times in Hollywood during the next few years, but they remained casual acquaintances until 1965, when they began dating after both of their marriages went on the rocks.

It was also in 1963 that Julie underwent psychoanalysis for the first time, which she would continue to do for the next 20 years. Despite her economic and artistic success and all of the trappings of her celebrity status, Julie was depressed and confused. The emotional traumas of her early years when her parents divorced, coupled with the drive to continually advance her career, and the insecurities and sometimes insensitive realities of show business, resulted in Julie's decision to seek professional counselling.

She took a few weeks off after the filming of *Emily* for a short reunion with Tony and Emma Kate back home. Then she had to rush back to Hollywood where *The Sound of Music* was to begin filming interior scenes at the Fox Studio. When she later left for Salzburg, Austria, to film the gorgeous hilltop scenes, she took Emma Kate with her.

Under the direction of Robert Wise (known for his Oscar-winning *West Side Story*, among other films), Julie's talent flourished. Wise and Julie shared the rare combination of perfectionism and efficiency that resulted in a highly professional end product without waste of time, effort, or money. Despite weather problems and other unexpected snafus, the film ran only three weeks over schedule, which was far below the norm for such a complex production.

Both before and during the filming, skeptics expressed doubt about the boxoffice potential of *Music*. The original Broadway production had not generally been considered one of Rodgers and Hammerstein's stronger efforts, and many observers felt that the material for the sugar-coated stage musical was too saccharine to be credible in the more realistic film medium.

Despite the thoroughly professional direction of Robert Wise and the flawless production values that were producing an awesome-looking film, 20th Century-Fox itself was not convinced that *Music* would be a surefire success. *Mary Poppins* had not been released yet, so Julie's boxoffice popularity was still an unknown quantity.

The studio's confidence was bolstered considerably when *Mary Poppins* was shown in some advance screenings in August 1964. Even before the world premiere, scheduled for the following month at New York's Radio City Music Hall, the word was out: Disney had discovered the newest film superstar.

When the film opened in New York and other metropolitan areas in September, the reviews were rapturous. Disney clearly had fulfilled his goal to outdo all of his past achievements. The boxoffice was booming, and Oscar talk was in the air. During the next few months, the film opened throughout the country, doing spectacular business everywhere it played.

Warners' *My Fair Lady* was released the following month, and it was equally well received. In a curious way, Julie's aura sort of clung to the *My Fair Lady* film phenomenon, even though she didn't appear in it. Critics and journalists often spoke of *Poppins* and *Lady* in the same breath, as both were lavish costume pieces set in roughly the same time and place. Even the *Poppins* score by Richard M. Sherman and Robert B. Sherman was said by some to be similar to Lerner and Loewe's tunes in *Lady*. The film musical was now having a sudden resurgence in popularity, courtesy of Julie's marvelous *Poppins* film debut and the film version of her most celebrated Broadway show. Fall 1964 was very much the season of Julie Andrews.

Ironically, Julie probably ended up with more sympathetic media publicity due to her *not* getting the role *in My Fair Lady* than if she had appeared in the film. Nonetheless, Julie had clearly been a phenomenon waiting to happen ever since she stepped off the plane in New York in 1954. Ten years later, the payoff had arrived.

In a limited sort of way, the momentum continued when *The Americanization of Emily* opened in November 1964 to mixed reviews. A sardonic antiwar satire was probably not ideal holiday season fare, and *Emily* was buried in the marketplace under the hoopla surrounding the two heavyweights, *Poppins* and *Lady*.

Julie received some good, if not stupendous reviews for her role as a World War II motor car driver in London who falls in love with a pacifistic Naval lieutenant. It was a definite career plus for her, but was not widely enough seen for Julie to reap much benefit in showcasing her dramatic abilities. This was unfortunate, because if the film had a higher profile, it might have counteracted a lot of the stereotypical thinking about Julie that had already started with the release of *Poppins*.

After the 1964 holiday season, the annual awards cycle began. On February 8, 1965, Julie accepted the Golden Globe Award for Best Actress in a Musical for *Mary Poppins*. At the conclusion of her acceptance speech, she delivered her now-famous quote, "I'd like to thank the man who made this all possible -- Jack Warner." It was refreshing to see that Mary Poppins was capable of a little calculated bitchiness.

Later that month, the Academy Awards nominations were announced. As expected, Julie was on the list of distinguished Best Actress nominees for her film debut in *Poppins*. In what was widely regarded as a deliberate snub, Audrey Hepburn was not on the list, although *My Fair Lady's* 12 nominations encompassed all of the major categories *except* Best Actress. The press felt that she was left out by Academy voters as a sympathetic gesture to Julie, for losing the *Lady* role. Meanwhile, *Mary Poppins* edged out *Lady* in the total nominations, receiving 13, including the first Best Picture nod in the Disney Studio's history.

As if this wasn't exciting enough, Julie would add two more milestones to her career before 1965 was half over. The first event was the one that clinched her stature as Hollywood's new boxoffice queen. *The Sound of Music* didn't just open on March 2. It sort of took off like a high-powered rocket, making instant movie history. The New York premiere was a celebrity-studded affair and received a fantastic audience response. As the film opened in major cities in time for the Easter holidays, it drew massive audiences. Then, as it gradually opened throughout the country, it quickly overtook *Gone With the Wind* as the highest-grossing film up to that time. (It held that title until the release of *Star Wars* in 1977.) The film soundtrack became the best-selling record album in history up to that time, replacing the Broadway cast recording of *My Fair Lady*.

To the great shock of 20th Century-Fox, the film received the most scathingly nasty reviews of any Julie Andrews vehicle since *Mountain Fire* in 1954. In most cases, thankfully, the critics had kind words for Julie herself. And there were a handful of major critics who adored the entire film.

The second career milestone of 1965 was the April Oscar ceremony, where attention was clearly focused on the supposed Julie/Audrey Hepburn rivalry. Audrey was to be the presenter of the Best Actor award, which Rex Harrison was heavily favored to win. The films themselves took a backseat to the more pressing question -- would Julie get her sweet revenge?

The answer was affirmative. Good-sport Julie accepted her award graciously, and even better-sport Audrey appeared to harbor no malice. The *Poppins* pot was sweetened with four other Oscars. *My Fair Lady* won the big prize, Best Picture, and Rex Harrison was victorious as Best Actor. *Lady* also collected six other awards.

Although she had been widely predicted as the likely Best Actress winner, some observers expressed surprise at Julie's win. Seldom in Academy history have acting prizes been handed out for musicals. The skeptics challenged Julie's win, arguing that it was merely a competent performance in a light, undemanding role. Whether anti-Warner sentiment played a part in Julie's victory was anybody's guess. In any case, Julie is a first-rate actress and *Poppins* required considerable skill, no matter how easy it may have appeared. The important fact was that the film industry had paid Julie its highest honor. She was clearly "in" among the press and her professional colleagues.

Now that Julie's first three movies had been released, she could breathe a little easier. The wait between the wrapup of filming and the release of the films had seemed interminable. But it had been worth the wait. She had found the acceptance she was hoping for -- in a big way.

However, Julie was also a hard-driving, self-motivated woman who didn't rest on her laurels. Now that she had reached fame and fortune by playing two prim and proper British nannies, she became concerned about the obvious identifications this would bring. She didn't feel comfortable in the role of America's prim and proper G-rated sweetheart and began looking for projects that would help to break that mold. The first such opportunity to come along was *Hawaii*, a multimillion-dollar United Artists Studio extravaganza based on a portion of James Michener's mammoth historical novel. Julie was to play Jerusa, a New England girl who married the religious fundamentalist Abner Hale and set sail with him for Hawaii, where his group of missionaries was travelling to educate the pagans and convert them to Christianity.

In a sense, the role was not a radical departure for Julie because Jerusa was a kind and properly bred young Protestant woman, not a character of questionable motives or weak moral fibre. However, this was a dramatic film, not a musical. Julie's part had more dimension and depth than her film musical roles had offered. Furthermore, it was a big-scale Hollywood project, allowing Julie to continue in the type of prestige vehicle reserved for filmdom's elite superstars.

Much of the picture was filmed on location in Honolulu, meaning Julie had another long separation from Tony, who was in Spain designing the film version of *A Funny Thing Happened on the Way to the Forum*. It was an exhausting experience, as Julie had to deal with the intense tropical heat and the difficult storm sequences in the film. However, it was a period of personal growth and reflection for Julie. She developed enduring friendships with director George Roy Hill (who also directed her in *Thoroughly Modern Millie*) and Max Von Sydow (who teamed with her again 20 years later in *Duet For One*).

Immediately after she completed *Hawaii*, she returned to Hollywood where she was beginning her next film at Universal Studio. The suspense thriller, *Torn Curtain*, appeared to be another coups for Julie. She was being directed by the renowned master of suspense, Alfred Hitchcock, and costarring with one of the hottest leading men of the 60s, Paul Newman. It was a moderately budgeted film, although Julie garnered her highest salary to date, $750,000 against a percentage of the gross.

Julie's second nonmusical in a row was heralded in the media as a complete departure for her. The press proclaimed that a planned seminude lovemaking scene between Julie and Newman, who were unmarried lovers in the film, would bury her Mary Poppins image forever. Unfortunately, the film was such a misfire that most audiences probably slept through the tepid bedroom scene. Julie and Newman had virtually no chemistry together and Hitchcock must have been bored, because it was one of his weakest efforts.

Following the triumphant Oscar win and the *Sound of Music's* success, Julie was under great pressure to keep her career momentum going. Although Tony's career was flourishing, Julie was still the superstar in the family. This began to put a strain on her marriage. Her earnings and her international fame easily eclipsed his. He was respected and admired among his peers, but hardly a well known celebrity like she was.

However, the biggest factor that made a healthy marriage impossible was clearly the geographical separation. Tony's growing number of film assignments kept him on the go to Spain, Sweden, San Francisco, and New York, while Julie's films also kept her on the move. Cliches to the contrary, this much absence doesn't make the heart grow fonder. As the press had been speculating for almost a year, the Waltons formally separated in Fall 1966.

Although *Hawaii* and *Torn Curtain* were both released in 1966, neither did much to advance Julie's career. Both films made fair profits. *Hawaii* had several good reviews, but few out-and-out raves. *Curtain* deservedly received mostly critical pans. Julie was better in *Hawaii* than she was in *Curtain*, because the part had more dimension. It would have been difficult for anyone to be more than passable in the dull *Curtain*.

Despite two unspectacular film efforts and her broken marriage, 1966 was not all bad news for Julie. In February, she received her second Best Actress nomination, for *The Sound of Music*. In March, she had the distinction of placing her hands and footprints in front of Graumann's Chinese Theatre in Hollywood, a routine but important ritual in the passage to Hollywood stardom.

Although she lost the Best Actress Oscar to Julie Christie in April, after having been heavily predicted as the winner, she was secure enough in her fame at this point to not be too disappointed. She was compensated somewhat when *Music* snatched the coveted Best Picture prize from the favored *Doctor Zhivago*, and picked up four other awards, including one for director Robert Wise.

In Summer 1966, Julie began work on her third movie musical, *Thoroughly Modern Millie* for producer Ross Hunter and her *Hawaii* mentor, George Roy Hill, directing at Universal. *Millie* was an opportunity for Julie to return to her musical comedy roots. Not only would she be able to sing and dance, but she also had some great slapstick bits to clown around in. Furthermore, the role was spunkier and less sticky-sweet than in her previous film musicals. She even got to vamp John Gavin, Theda Bara-style in one hilarious sequence. It was a superb opportunity to stretch her comic talents, and she attacked it with relish.

The movie was a major boxoffice success for Universal when it premiered in 1967, the top grosser in the studio's history. Once again, Julie was breaking records everywhere she went. It seemed every producer in Hollywood wanted to star Julie in a picture. In 1965, she had been named the top boxoffice draw in America by the National Theatre owners. In 1966 and 1967, she held the top spot. In 1968, she was in the third spot.

In 1969, she fell off the top 10 list and never appeared on it again. For, with the release of her next two films, *Star!* (1968) and *Darling Lili* (1970), the bottom fell out, and her reign at the top of the Hollywood heap was over as fast as it had begun.

Prior to this sudden turn in fortune for Julie's career, her personal life had been reasonably happy. Her years in analysis had helped her tremendously in dealing with her problems. Her splitup with Tony Walton was amicable, and the possibility of a reconciliation still existed. Julie split her time between filmmaking in Hollywood and relaxing with 5-year old Emma Kate in the house that the family had purchased near Beverly Hills.

Julie's half-brother, Chris, lived with her and Emma for a couple of years while he studied photography in Los Angeles. The diehard English girl had grown fond of Hollywood and was enjoying the material rewards of her hard-earned success. She spent her spare time reading poetry, oil painting, enjoying classical music, and entertaining Emma Kate.

In 1966, Julie and Blake Edwards began seeing each other more frequently. Edwards' career was in a slump at the time. He was ending a bitter marriage to Patricia Walker, with divorce pending. He purchased a new home in Malibu. He and Julie spent time between his new home, her place in Beverly Hills, and vacations in Switzerland, which they both adored.

The romance was becoming more serious, but Julie was still officially married to Tony Walton, and a new marriage didn't appear to be in her immediate plans. Julie became very close to Edwards' two children, Geoffrey and Jennifer, who were, respectively, 10 and 7 years old at the time.

In February, 1967, Julie began work on her next film, *Star!*, a lavish, expensive musical that 20th Century-Fox hoped would duplicate the *Sound of Music* success. The biography of British stage star Gertrude Lawrence, who died in 1952, was to be assembled by most of the creative team who had worked on *Music*, most notably director Robert Wise. Wise had been planning the project for three years, having first discussed the role with Julie in 1964.

Everything about the production was to be first-class. Incorporating songs from many of the great composers of musical theatre (Gershwin, Weill, Porter and others), this was envisioned as the musical to outclass all musicals, and everyone was anticipating another monster success for Julie.

The part of Gertrude Lawrence offered Julie her greatest acting challenge yet. The boisterous, egocentric, alcoholic, eccentric Lawrence was about as far removed from Julie as two people could get. Julie and Gertrude were both British and they both worked their way up from the English music halls to achieve international stardom. But the real resemblance ended there.

Both Julie and Wise smartly agreed to avoid trying an actual impersonation of Lawrence, instead trying to suggest the colorful climate and temperament of her life -- a canvas interpretation of the spirit of her life without pretensions to exact replication.

It was during the strenuous and difficult filming of this complex, multimillion dollar production that Julie filed for divorce from Tony Walton, on November 14, 1967. Everyone assumed that this was a signal for an upcoming Andrews/Edwards merger announcement.

No such announcement came. However, a different kind of Andrews/ Edwards merger was announced. Edwards was to direct Julie in *Darling Lili*, a

World War I musical with an espionage background. Edwards' long-time collaborator, Henry Mancini, and Johnny Mercer created several new songs for Julie.

The big-budget Paramount release, costarring Rock Hudson, was to film in Paris, Hollywood, Brussells, and Dublin. Julie was to paid more than a million dollars for her services.

Filming began in Hollywood in March, 1968. Shortly thereafter, the company travelled to Europe to begin the location footage. Things went relatively smoothly in Ireland, but in Paris and Brussells, a series of problems began -- everything from bureaucratic snafus banning the use of planned locations to uncooperative weather. Before long, the film was millions of dollars over budget and way behind schedule.

When *Star!* had its world premiere in London in July, 1968, Julie was not allowed to attend, as scheduled. Paramount was shelling out in excess of $70,000 per day to keep the company in Europe. Finally, the studio forced Edwards to return to Hollywood to complete the picture.

This was the beginning of the bad media rap that Julie got from the press, a near-vendetta that was to cause her grief for the next several years. She was severely reprimanded for not attending the *Star!* premiere, being termed ungrateful to the public that had made her a star.

An unending series of reports from the set accused Edwards of waste and egotistical, irresponsible extravagance. He was reportedly making a $15-million home movie starring his lady love, with Paramount picking up the tab.

The Hollywood press seems to relish tales of impending doom for big-budget movies, as it makes for good copy. More than a year before it was released, *Darling Lili* was being described by journalists as a big enough bomb to sink Paramount Pictures, much like *Cleopatra* almost did to 20th Century-Fox in 1963.

At this point, Julie desperately needed an artistic triumph to shake up the bitterly negative press off their high horse and back down to earth. But luck was obviously not on Julie's side. When *Star!* opened its roadshow engagements in October, 1968, it was massacred by several major critics. And those that didn't massacre it damned it with faint praise. The biggest insult was the *New York Times*' 250-word review, where sheer brevity in covering such an eagerly awaited, expensive film was the clearest possible dismissal of the entire film.

Worse yet, the audiences did not come to the rescue this time, as they had for *The Sound of Music*. The film died quickly in it roadshow engagements. In a desperate move, Fox yanked the film from release, re-edited it in a shorter version called *Those Were the Happy Times*, and re-released it with ads that made it look like a sticky-sweet bon bon. But the film was dead as a doornail. Audiences still rejected it.

Meanwhile, Julie and Edwards had wrapped up *Darling Lili*, and Edwards was battling with Paramount over the final cut of the film. Paramount felt that it had $15 million dollars worth of pretty scenery and a few fetching scenes, but no coherent film. The release was pushed back from late 1969 to mid-1970, a sure sign to film exhibitors that Paramount believed it had a turkey.

Amidst the shocking turn of events in Julie's career, she sought to solidify her personal life. She married Blake Edwards on November 12 1969 in a private ceremony at Julie's home in Beverly Hills, where Blake and his two children had already moved in. Shortly thereafter, the couple had a larger house built for them in Beverly Hills and also purchased a getaway house on Malibu Beach.

The event that finally dealt the fatal blow to Julie's film career occurred when *Darling Lili* opened in Summer 1970. The majority of the reviews were devastatingly nasty, and Julie's audience had apparently deserted her again. After the double whammy of *Star!* and *Darling Lili*, Julie was no longer considered a good boxoffice bet. Two musicals planned for her at MGM, *She Loves Me* and *Say it with Music*, were cancelled. And no other offers appeared to be forthcoming.

Julie did not appear in another film for the next five years. As of this writing, she has only done two films that were not directed by Blake Edwards. She turned to television in the early 1970's. She did an NBC-TV variety special with Harry Belafonte that aired in November, 1969. In 1971, she reteamed with Carol Burnett for *Julie and Carol at Lincoln Center*, a two-person musical variety show on CBS-TV, similar to their first outing, but not quite as good.

Then Julie took the plunge into series television. She made a lucrative deal with Sir Lew Grade, whose ITV Productions was to produce at least 24 episodes of *The Julie Andrews Hour*, a musical variety show for weekly airing in England and the U.S., supplemented by one film per year as long as the series was running. It was a good opportunity for Julie to try to cultivate a new audience for herself, perhaps slowly rebuilding her tarnished reputation in films.

The series premiered in the U.S. on ABC-TV in September 1972, featuring such guest stars as Robert Goulet, Joel Grey, James Stewart, Carl Reiner, Angela Lansbury, and Henry Mancini. The show won extravagant praise from most critics in both nations, and won several Emmy awards. However, the ratings were not high enough for ABC to keep the series alive past its one-season commitment to ITC. After having worked extremely hard for more than a year, Julie had to face another painful career disappointment.

The one film that Sir Lew Grade owed Julie as a part of their deal was released in 1974. *The Tamarind Seed* was an exotic spy picture costarring Omar Sharif. It was a respectable effort but had little impact. Julie handled her role as competently as ever, but it was not a vehicle with enough energy for anyone to care.

With both of their careers stalled, Julie and Blake had scant reason to remain in Hollywood. They moved their family to Switzerland in June 1973 and purchased a house in London as well.

Julie's brief stint as an author of children's books, *Mandy* (1971) and *The Last of the Really Great Whangdoodles* (1974) gave her pleasure, but neither was a commercial or critical success. A third book, *Babe*, was begun in 1984 but, as of this writing, has not been released. She is reportedly planning to write her autobiography in the near future.

Julie has also devoted some of her time to various charities, including the Hathaway House for disabled boys in Hollywood and the Committee of Responsibility, an organization sponsoring medical treatment for children injured in the Viet Nam War. As a result of this, she and Blake adopted two young Viet Nam orphans, Amy and Joanna.

In 1976, Julie enjoyed a successful concert engagement at the London Palladium, where she had appeared in the early years of her career. However, a concert stint at Caesar's Palace the same year proved unsuccessful for her. In 1977, she organized a successful concert tour that took her to several U.S. cities and to Japan.

The first film offer after *The Tamarind Seed* that interested her was Blake Edwards' *10*, a well received 1979 satiric comedy that costarred Dudley Moore and Bo Derek.

Throughout the 1980s, she worked sparingly. In 1980, she did her first film without Edwards since *Star!* It was the undistinguished *Little Miss Marker*, in which she played a supporting role to Walter Matthau and Sara Stimson, an adorable young moppet.

In 1981, she appeared in *S.O.B.*, Edwards' long-planned attack against Hollywood, including Julie's celebrated (and embarrassing) bare breast scene. The film had some admirers among critics, but audiences obviously didn't want to see Mary Poppins' nipples.

Her biggest personal film triumph since *Thoroughly Modern Millie* was *Victor/Victoria* in 1982, Edwards' hilarious sexual masquerade farce. This film returned Julie to the world of musicals, rave reviews, powerful boxoffice, and even Academy Award recognition (a Best Actress nomination), but curiously did not reactivate her film career.

Her next film certainly didn't help in that regard. The less said about *The Man Who Loved Women*, a muddled comedy costarring Burt Reynolds and directed by Edwards, the better.

In 1986, she returned to form in two impressive performances, another Edwards film (*That's Life!*) and a non-Edwards film, (*Duet For One*). Despite rave reviews for her demanding dramatic performances in both of these films (including critical rallying for Best Actress Oscar nominations, to no avail), the result has not been a surge of attractive new film offers. As of this writing, she hasn't been in a film since *Duet For One*.

Throughout the 80's, Julie has made a lot of personal appearances, often for charitable organizations. In Los Angels, she has performed in benefit concerts for Operation California, a disaster relief organization. At the amphitheatre next to Universal Studio in Hollywood, she and Placido Domingo gave a 1986 benefit concert to aid victims of the 1986 Mexico earthquake. She also appeared in a benefit for the John French Foundation for Alzheimer's Disease.

She returned to Japan for a successful concert tour in early 1980. In 1987, after a 5-year absent from the concert stage, she successfully performed tour of seven major U.S. cities, earning mostly favorable reviews.

She continues to do television specials (such as the *American Film Institute Salute to Jack Lemmon* in 1988 and an Emmy-winning 1987 Christmas special). At this writing, another reunion special for Julie and Carol Burnett is reportedly in the works for ABC-TV.

Earlier talks of a stage musical based on the *Victor/Victoria* film fell through, but Julie is said to be considering a return to the stage in a revival of Kurt Weill's *Lady in the Dark*, initially for London and perhaps eventually for Broadway. (*Lady in the Dark* was one of Gertrude Lawrence's starring vehicles. Julie's climactic number in *Star!* [see Filmography entry **F06**], a biography of Gertrude Lawrence, is Julie's rendition of "Jenny" from *Lady in the Dark*.) Even if the stage productions of *Dark* don't materialize, a special studio recording of the show's musical score is scheduled for Julie in England as this book goes to press.

Her stepchildren, Jennifer Edwards and Geoffrey Edwards are pursuing careers as an actress and film editor, respectively. (Both have worked in these capacities in Blake Edwards' films. Her daughter, Emma Kate Walton, is a budding actress, having appeared as the daughter of Julie and Jack Lemmon in *That's Llfe!* Her adopted children, Amy and Joanne, are now in their teens and reside with Julie and Edwards in Gstaad, Switzerland.

The Edwards still have a house in Malibu, but spend most of their time at their Swiss villa. Edwards continues to work on film projects, such as *Sunset* (1988), starring James Garner and Bruce Willis, and *Skin Deep* (1989), starring John Ritter.

As has been the case for the past several years, Julie now considers her husband and children her top priorities. Show business projects are something to occasionally, whenever something interesting enough pops up.

Julie, James Garner, and Joyce Grenfel in MGM's *The Americanization of Emily.* (1964)

Julie in the famous opening scene in the Austrian Alps in 20th Century-Fox's *The Sound of Music*. (1965)

Julie, Max Von Sydow, Lou Antonio, and Lane Bradbury in United Artists' *Hawaii*. (1966)

Julie with Mary Tyler Moore in Universal's *Thoroughly Modern Millie*. (1967)

Julie in the "Parisian Pierrot" number from 20th Century-Fox's *Star!* (1968)

Director Gower Champion, Julie, and Harry Belafonte rehearsing the NBC-TV special, *An Evening With Julie Andrews and Harry Belafonte.* (1969)

Julie as spy Lili Smith in Paramount's *Darling Lili*. (1970)

Julie prepares for the debut of her first television series, ABC-TV's *The Julie Andrews Hour.* (1972)

Julie recreates her *My Fair Lady* role of Eliza Doolittle in the premiere episode of ABC-TV's *The Julie Andrews Hour.* (1972)

Julie reprises her "Burlington Bertie From Bow" routine from *Star!* in the premiere episode of ABC-TV's *The Julie Andrews Hour*. (1972)

Julie, Ken Barry, and chorus in a spoof of Fred Astaire/Ginger Rogers movies in ABC-TV's *The Julie Andrews Hour.* (1972)

Julie as she appeared in Orion Pictures' *10* starring Dudley Moore. (1979)

Robert Preston and Julie sing "You and Me" in MGM's *Victor/Victoria.* (1982)

Julie as a concert violinist in Cannon Films' *Duet For One*. (1986)

Chronology

October 1, 1935	Julia Elizabeth Wells was born in Walton-on Thames, Surrey, England.
1943	Sang in an air raid shelter in Beckenham where her stepfather, Ted Andrews, led community singing during air raids. (Julie's voice conspicuously soared an octave or two above everyone else's.)
1945	Began singing in her parents' vaudeville act.
December 5, 1946	Sang with her parents at the Stage Door Canteen, Piccadilly, London. The Queen Mother and Princess Margaret were in attendance.
1947	First screen test at M-G-M in London.
October 22, 1947	Sang in the *Starlight Roof* revue at the London Hippodrome, which ran for several months
November 1, 1948	Command performance at the London Palladium.
Christmas, 1948	Played in *Aladdin* and *Humpty Dumpty* at the London Casino, where she first met her future husband, Tony Walton.
Christmas, 1953	Played the title role in *Cinderella* at the London Palladium.
August 23, 1954	Boarded a plane for her first trip to America to begin rehearsals for *The Boy Friend*.

September 30, 1954	Her Broadway debut: *The Boy Friend* opened to favorable reviews.
March, 15, 1956	*My Fair Lady*, costarring Rex Harrison, opened on Broadway to rave reviews.
March 24, 1956	Recorded the original cast album of *My Fair Lady* at CBS Studios in New York.
March 31, 1957	Rodgers and Hammerstein's *Cinderella* premiered as a CBS-TV original musical special starring Julie and Jon Cypher.
April 30, 1958	*My Fair Lady* had its British premiere at London's Drury Lane Theatre, starring Julie and the principal original cast from Broadway.
February 1, 1959	The London cast of *My Fair Lady* recorded the original London cast album for Columbia.
May 10, 1959	Married Tony Walton.
December 3, 1960	*Camelot*, costarring Richard Burton and Robert Goulet, opened on Broadway to mixed reviews.
June, 1962	*Julie and Carol at Carnegie Hall*, an Emmy-winning CBS-TV musical variety special, costarring Carol Burnett, was aired.
November 27, 1962	Emma Kate Walton was born to Julie and Tony Walton.
September, 1964	First film, *Mary Poppins*, opened to critical raves.
November, 1964	Film *The Americanization of Emily*, costarring James Garner, opened to generally favorable reviews.
February, 1965	Received her first Best Actress Oscar nomination for *Mary Poppins*.
February 8, 1965	Received the Golden Globe Award for Best Actress in a Musical (*Mary Poppins*).
March 2, 1965	Film *The Sound of Music* opened to mixed reviews and record-breaking boxoffice returns.
April 5, 1965	Won the Best Actress Oscar for *Mary Poppins*.
February, 1966	Received her second Best Actress Oscar nomination (for *Sound of Music*).

March 26, 1966	Placed an imprint of her hands and feet in the cement in front of Grauman's Chinese Theatre in Hollywood.
April 8, 1966	At the Academy Awards ceremony in Los Angeles, she lost as Best Actress for *The Sound of Music* to Julie Christie (*Darling*).
July, 1966	Alfred Hitchcock's *Torn Curtain*, teaming Julie with Paul Newman, opened to negative reviews.
October, 1966	Film *Hawaii*, costarring Max von Sydow, opened to mixed reviews.
March, 1967	Film *Thoroughly Modern Millie* opened to mixed reviews.
November 14, 1967	Filed for divorce from Tony Walton.
April, 1968	Appeared at the Academy Awards ceremony in Los Angeles and presented the Best Picture Oscar for *In the Heat of the Night*.
July, 1968	Film *Star!* had its world premiere in London to fairly good reviews.
October, 1968	Film *Star!* opened in the U.S. metropolitan areas to mixed reviews.
November 13, 1969	Married Blake Edwards.
March, 1970	Julie's first film with Blake Edwards, *Darling Lili*, opened to mostly negative reviews; disastrous boxoffice results followed.
September, 1972	*The Julie Andrews Hour*, a weekly variety series, premiered on ABC-TV to rave reviews; it was to continue through April 1973.
September, 1974	Film *The Tamarind Seed*, costarring Omar Sharif, opened to mixed reviews.
September, 1979	Film *10*, costarring Dudley Moore and Bo Derek, opened to mostly good reviews.
October 5, 1979	Julie Andrews Day in Hollywood. After a ceremony, Julie received a star on the sidewalk in Hollywood Boulevard's Walk of Fame.
March, 1980	Film *Little Miss Marker*, costarring Walter Matthau, opened to lukewarm reviews.

July, 1981

Blake Edwards' film, *S.O.B.*, opened to widely divided reviews. It included Julie's highly publicized bare-breast scene.

March, 1982

Film *Victor/Victoria* opened to Julie's best reviews for film acting since *Thoroughly Modern Millie.*

February 1983

Received her third Best Actress Oscar nomination (for *Victor/Victoria*).

April, 1983

Lost her third Best Actress Oscar bid to Meryl Streep (*Sophie's Choice*).

December, 1983

Film *The Man Who Loved Women*, costarring Burt Reynolds, opened to negative reviews.

September, 1986

Film *That's Life*, costarring Jack Lemmon, received a mixed reaction, but excellent reviews for Julie.

December, 1986

Film *Duet For One*, costarring Alan Bates and Max von Sydow, opened to mixed reviews.

Filmography

F01　　　*MARY POPPINS*
　　　　　(Disney/Buena Vista; 1964; 140 minutes; Video: Disney)

Credits
Based on *Mary Poppins* books by P. L. Travers

Director	Robert Stevenson
Producer	Walt Disney
Coproducer	Bill Walsh
Screenplay	Bill Walsh, Don DaGradi
Original Song Score	Richard M. Sherman
	Robert B. Sherman
Orchestration	Irwin Kostal
Camera (Technicolor)	Edward Coleman
Editor	Cotton Warburton
Assistant Directors	Joseph L. McEveety
	Paul Feiner
Animation Director	Hamilton S. Luske

Cast

Mary Poppins	Julie Andrews
Bert	Dick Van Dyke
Mr. Banks	David Tomlinson
Mrs. Banks	Glynis Johns
Ellen	Hermoine Baddley
Jane Banks	Karen Dotrice
Michael Banks	Matthew Garber
Kate Nanna	Elsa Lanchester
Uncle Albert	Ed Wynn
Bird Woman	Jane Darwell
Constable Jones	Arthur Treacher
Admiral Boom	Reginald Owen
Mrs. Brill	Reta Shaw
Mr. Dawes, Jr.	Arthur Malet
Mr. Grubbs	Cyril Delevanti
Mr. Tomes	Lester Matthews

Mr. Mousley	Clive L. Halliday
Mr. Binnacle	Don Barclay
Miss Lark	Marjorie Bennett
Mrs. Corey	Alma Lawton
Miss Persimmon	Marjorie Eaton

Synopsis

In Edwardian London, Jane and Michael Banks are two precocious children who have trouble keeping a nanny to watch over them due to their mischevious ways. Their father, a bank executive, and their mother, a crusading suffragette, devote little time and attention to the moppets, so a warm, but firm, live-in nanny is required.

Lo and behold, an extraordinary nanny with an airborne umbrella literally flies into town to apply for the position, and readily accepts the job. What the curmudgeonly Mr. Banks doesn't realize is that his outspoken new governess is truly a magical person, bringing with her an abundance of incredible capabilities that will sweep the Banks children off their feet.

With her old pal Bert, the chimney sweep, she takes the children on some fanciful journeys, including a walk directly into a sidewalk-painted countryside, which comes alive as you step into it, and a tea party on the ceiling with Bert's cheerful Uncle Albert, where all of the guests are floating in mid-air. Mr. Banks is very skeptical of these seemingly nonsensical adventures that the children are telling him about, and decides to follow Mary Poppins' advice to take them with him to the bank for a lesson in practical frugality.

As Mr. Banks urges the children to deposit their tuppence in a bank account, a boisterous mixup occurs, causing the various customers to believe there's a run on the bank. This results in a widespread withdrawal of funds and eventually Banks' dismissal from his prestigious position.

Banks blames Poppins for all of the troubles in his household, but the kind chimney sweep Bert convinces him otherwise. Banks changes his stuffy attitude towards running his household, and is reinstated in his position at the bank. A climactic dance of the chimney sweeps above the rooftops of London sets the stage for a grand finale. As soon as Mary Poppins sees that everything is happy again in the Banks household, she positions her umbrella and sails away on a breeze, presumably to look for another unhappy household waiting to be set straight by her special brand of magic.

For a list of musical numbers, see the Discography section **(D15)**.

Commentary

Few film careers have started off quite as auspiciously as Julie Andrews'. Winning widespread critical acclaim and a Best Actress Oscar her very first time at bat, Julie was an instant movie superstar. The union between Broadway's fair Julie and Hollywood's magical Walt Disney in Julie's debut film proved a happy combination. The film was Disney's biggest boxoffice hit up to that time, and gave *My Fair Lady* a run for its money at the Academy Awards, collecting five Oscars to *Lady's* eight.

(This somewhat made up for the uproar caused in the industry by Jack Warner's passing up of Julie for the screen version of *Lady*, giving Julie's plum stage role to Audrey Hepburn.)

In the early 60s, the film musical was already on its last legs -- at least as far as mass audience popularity was concerned. With *Mary Poppins* -- and to an even greater extent, *The Sound of Music* (1965) -- Julie became the strongest possible argument for keeping the musical genre alive. The one-two boxoffice punch that Julie provided in *Mary Poppins* and *The Sound of Music* revitalized the ailing musical genre.

The role of the "practically perfect," prim and proper airborne governess fit Julie like a glove, and the film did full justice to the classic series of children's books by P. L. Travers, on which it was based. The only downside to this triumphant debut performance was the way it stereotyped Julie, coming back to haunt her in the years to follow, as Hollywood hesitated to cast her in more diverse roles.

Dick Van Dyke costarred as the chimney sweep Bert in a heartwarming story that skillfully blended live action special effects with vintage Disney animation. Such seasoned actors as Ed Wynn, Glynis Johns, David Tomlinson, Hermoine Baddley, and Elsa Lanchester added to the merriment.

Veteran Disney tunesmiths, Richard M. Sherman and Robert B. Sherman, composed one of their wittiest scores for the film, giving the fanciful tale appeal for adults as well as children. Gorgeous production values, glittering special effects, and a picture-postcard fairy tale view of Edwardian England added to the unalloyed delights.

The film was clearly an attempt by Disney to have his family films enter the big league and be taken seriously, and the 13 Oscar nominations by the Motion Picture Academy clearly demonstrated that his painstaking effort had paid off.

For years following *Poppins*, the Disney Studio tried to find another musical extravaganza to match the *Poppins* magic, but effort after effort (*Bedknobs and Broomsticks, The Happiest Millionaire, Pete's Dragon*) failed to meet the *Poppins* standard. Julie was courted to appear in several of these efforts (including a proposed *Poppins II*), but perhaps wisely declined. *Mary Poppins* was a once-in-a-lifetime melding of talents into a perfect artistic whole. And Julie, conquering Hollywood as the new boxoffice queen, was at the forefront of the spectacular success and excitement.

Reviews

Variety (9/2/64) -- The first major review on *Poppins* delivered the unqualified rave that Disney had hoped for. The review stated that the film brought the Disney magic to life "with eloquent and delicious lustre." The film was called "a stimulating cinematic experience...a must-see." Asserting that Disney had outdone himself in his latest effort, the review was especially complementary to Julie, calling her a "shining new film star" who "responds with bright veracity and fine voice." Robert Stevenson's direction of the film was termed "sensitive and understanding."

New York Times (9/25/64) -- Calling the film "a most wonderful, cheering movie," the review termed Julie's performance "superb" and the film itself "irresistible." Comparing *Poppins* to *My Fair Lady*, the review considered such a similarity "not unflattering to either." Dick Van Dyke was termed "joyous" as Bert, and Ed Wynn was called "grand" as Uncle Albert. Robert Stevenson's direction was praised for its inventiveness and "true Mary Poppins flair."

*****

F02   *THE AMERICANIZATION OF EMILY*
(MGM; 1964; 117 minutes; Video: None)

Credits

Based on the novel by William Bradford Huie

Director	Arthur Hiller
Producer	Martin Ransohoff
Screenplay	Paddy Chayefsky
Camera	Philip Lathrop
Editor	Tom McAdoo
Music	Johnny Mandel
Song ("Emily")	Johnny Mercer
Associate Producer	John Calley

Costumes	Bill Thomas
Assistant Director	Al Shenberg

Cast

Lt. Cmdr. Charles Madison	James Garner
Emily Barham	Julie Andrews
Admiral William Jessup	Melvyn Douglas
Lt. Cmdr. "Bus" Cummings	James Coburn
Mrs. Barham	Joyce Grenfel
Admiral Thomas Healy	Edward Binns
Sheila	Liz Fraser
Old Sailor	Keenan Wynn
Capt. Harry Spaulding	William Windom
Chief Petty Officer Paul Adams	John Crawford
Capt. Marvin Ellender	Douglas Henderson
Admiral Hoyle	Edmond Ryan
Young Sailor	Steve Franken
Gen. William Hallerton	Paul Newlan
Lt. Victor Wade	Gary Cockrell
Enright	Alan Sues
Port Commander	Bill Fraser
Nurse Captain	Lou Byrne
Port Ensign	Alan Howard
Pat	Linda Marlow
Nameless Broads	Janine Gray
	Judy Carne
	Kathy Kersh

Synopsis

Lt. Cmdr. Charles Madison is an American Naval officer stationed in London just before D Day in 1944. Much to his satisfaction, he has one of wartime's safest assignments. He is a "dog robber" for crusty old Admiral William Jessup. This means that his primary (though unofficial) duty is to keep the old codger supplied with ample booze, ample dining pleasures, ample women, and whatever else strikes his fancy. Since Madison is an avowed pacifist, this type of military assignment suits him just fine.

When Madison meets Emily Barham, a pretty young British war widow who serves the Navy as a motor car driver, a rapid romance develops between the two of them. However, as Emily lost both her husband and a brother in battle, she and her mother are deeply offended when Madison expresses his philosophies on war to them over tea. He expresses the viewpoint that wars will only cease when people stop thinking fighting wars is noble -- dead heroes are simply dead while living cowards are actually smarter (if not nobler).

Sooner than he realizes, Lt. Madison will have the opportunity to put his philosophies to the test. Admiral Jessup is concerned that the Army is getting all of the favorable media attention, while the Navy gets the short shrift. He concocts a dangerous and rather selfish ploy to gain his outfit some overdue publicity. He intends to send Lt. Madison to Omaha Beach to make a film of the upcoming Normandy invasion, as the Navy demolition team makes their landing. Worse yet, he is determined that the first dead man on Omaha Beach will be from the Navy.

Madison balks at the foolhardy scheme, but is told in no uncertain terms by the Admiral that he has no choice in the matter. Certain that the idea is too ridiculous to ever occur, Madison brushes it aside and turns his attentions to courting Emily. Despite their differing opinions on the valor of war, Emily finds herself falling in love and accepts Madison's marriage proposal.

Soon thereafter, Madison discovers that amidst his publicity-seeking campaign, Admiral Jessup has promised the discussed film footage to the President, who is very pleased and anxious to see the film. Meanwhile, Jessup has a complete mental breakdown. While it's clear to those around Jessup that his plans were set forth in a fit of madness, things have progressed too far to turn back. It seems that the insane assignment for Madison will become a reality after all. Madison has a date with a camera on the D Day battlefield.

Madison is at first distraught, then jubilant, when he discovers that due to a scheduling snafu he will miss reaching the departure point for Normandy by a couple of hours. Noticing his glib mood as he departs, Emily knows something is up. She feels Madison's selfishness and cowardice are obscene in view of the fact that many men will be killed. She tells Madison off and says she never wants to see him again as he boards the plane.

Madison's snug complacency that he will avoid the invasion turns to stark terror when he discovers that the departure had to be delayed due to weather complications. He will definitely be able to accompany the batallion, accompanied by his friend, Lt. Cmdr. Bus Cummings.

During the battle, it appears that Madison is killed. Cummings returns to London with the news that Madison was the first man to be killed on Omaha Beach. The media goes wild promoting this celebrated war hero, just about the time Admiral Jessup improves and does not remember having made the foolhardy assignment. He is shocked this his foolish plan was carried out and remorseful that Madison died because of it.

Just then Madison shows up in a hospital in France and is preparing to return to London. Everyone is stunned and delighted by the news, but Jessup is especially jubilant. This is even more heroic than a dead sailor. It's a *presumed* dead sailor who wasn't dead after all. Madison is to be decorated for his bravery and valor.

Cummings reveals to Emily that Madison wasn't brave at all. He was running the opposite direction from the battle. Cummings had to literally drag him to the scene. The entire affair had been a gigantic hoax.

When Madison returns, Emily is so happy to see him that she brushes idealistic differences aside and again pledges her love to him. In a sudden switch, Madison becomes virtuous and pious. He vows to tell the truth to the news media and bring the Navy to ridicule, sacrificing his own career and the benefits of his status as a decorated hero in the process. Emily points out that this is opposite his own previously espoused philosophy. Now she has come full circle to Madison's viewpoint, valuing human life and happiness above pious principles. She has switched from a sanctimonious British hawk to a pacifistic American dove. Realizing that Emily is right, Madison decides to bask in the glory of his sudden change of fortune. Marrying and settling down with Emily will be a much better fate than sitting around in the brig feeling righteous and noble.

Commentary

Largely overlooked in the spectacular 1964/65 movie season (of *Mary Poppins/My Fair Lady/The Sound of Music*), *The Americanization of Emily* was a film that had its own share of cult devotees. A black-and-white antiwar satire with a sardonic Paddy Chayefsky screenplay might have seemed more an art house item than a major studio year-end release. But that's without considering the presence of the ever-popular James Garner and Julie, right on the heels of her *Mary Poppins* triumph. When Julie was initially cast by MGM, no one could have predicted what a fortuitous move her casting would prove to be.

As they demonstrated again 18 years later in *Victor/Victoria*, Andrews and Garner make a terrific starring team. Their sparkling performances, in fact, keep this sometimes cynical and unpleasant tale of human vice from turning sour.

This was the earliest display of Julie's talents in a straight comedy or drama film, and the seriocomic nature of the material allowed her a full range of emotions. When one considers the subsequent battle she fought for several years to shed her image as a goody-goody star of children's movies, one can only surmise that most people of that mindset did not see this movie. She plays an enlisted motor car driver during World War II, and the role is sexy, provocative, and quite challenging.

Backed by a superb cast, including Melvyn Douglas as a deranged Navy admiral, Joyce Grenfel as Julie's mother, grieving for a son killed in battle, and James Coburn's hilarious turn as Garner's on again/ off again buddy Lt. Commander Bus Cummings, this was a first-class production all the way. Splendid production values, including the climactic expertly photographed battle sequences, added to the enjoyment. And the Paddy Chayefsky script was wittier, more literate, intelligent, and challenging than the typical Hollywood assembly line romantic comedy. Though not as popular as her musicals, Julie's second film clearly added impetus to her rapidly escalating superstar status in the mid-60s.

Reviews

Variety (10/28/64) -- Providing a mixed critique, this major trade paper felt that the film had "its glaring faults as well as its virtues." Although the film was said to carry "a certain breeziness," the reviewer felt that some aspects of the story would be "hard to stomach" for many viewers. The reviewer considered strong selling points to be "the reappearance of Julie Andrews...and James Garner in another...light comedy role." The romance between their characters was said to be the film's primary interest. Julie was said to display "a charming presence...Part enables her both comedy and dramatic rendition." Garner was said to sometimes force his scenes but to "generally deliver a satisfactory performance." Arthur Hiller's direction was said to maintain "a swift pace."

New York Times (10/28/64) -- This review praised the film for giving Julie a chance to "prove herself irresistible in a straight romantic comedy." The material was said to achieve "some of the wildest, brashest, and funniest situations and cracks at the lunacy of warfare" to be seen in a film. The performances of both Julie and Garner were termed "splendid." The work of supporting players James Coburn, Melvyn Douglas, and Edward Binns was called "dandy." The "spinning comedy" was also admired for its intellectual commentary on "basic pacifism."

*****

F03   ***THE SOUND OF MUSIC***
                 (20th-Century Fox; 1965; 174 minutes; Video:CBS/Fox)

Credits
Based on the stageplay by Howard Lindsay and Russell Crouse

Producer/Director	Robert Wise
Screenplay	Ernest Lehman
Lyrics	Oscar Hammerstein II
Music and Additional Lyrics	Richard Rodgers
Orchestration	Irwin Kostal
Production Design	Boris Leven
Camera (DeLuxe Color)	Ted McCord
Editor	William Reynolds
Assistant Director	Ridgeway Callow
Sound	Murray Spivack
	Bernard Freericks

Cast

Maria	Julie Andrews
Captain Von Trapp	Christopher Plummer
Baroness	Eleanor Parker
Max Detweiler	Richard Haydn
Mother Abbess	Peggy Wood
Liesl	Charmian Carr
Louisa	Heather Menzies
Frederich	Nicolas Hammond
Kurt	Duane Chase
Brigitta	Angela Cartwright
Marta	Debbie Turner
Gretl	Kym Karath
Sister Margaretta	Anna Lee
Sister Berthe	Portia Nelson
Herr Zeller	Ben Wright
Rolfe	Daniel Truhitte
Frau Schmidt	Norma Varden
Franz	Gil Stuart
Sister Sophia	Marni Nixon
Sister Bernice	Evadne Baker
Baroness Ebberfeld	Doris Lloyd
Songs for Christopher Plummer	Bill Lee
Songs for Peggy Wood	Marjorie McKay

Synopsis

The story is loosely based on the real adventures of the Trapp Family singers, who fled Austria in the early days of World War II to evade the Nazi movement, which was taking over their homeland.

Maria is a postulant in an nun's abbey in pre-World War II Austria. She has vowed to become a nun, but she has a defiant spirit and a penchant for mischief that makes the kindly Mother Superior wonder whether she's ready for a life devoted to God.

To give Maria a chance to decide, the Mother Superior sends her out of the abbey to become the governess of a retired Naval Captain who is a widow with seven children. Maria reluctantly follows the Mother Superior's command.

Maria does not approve of the overly strict way that the Captain runs his home, and is outspoken enough to let him know it, much to his irritation. But she has a quick empathy with the children, who she teaches to sing, takes on excursions, and provides a good dose of the fun they had been missing since their mother died.

A snooty Baroness enters the picture. Much to the children's dismay, the Captain announces that he is engaged to the Baroness. The reaction is even stronger for Maria, who suddenly realizes she is falling in love with the Captain. When challenged by the Baroness (who senses a budding romance), she returns to the Abbey, confused and feeling guilty about her emotions.

The Mother Superior recognizes a continuing restlessness in Maria and urges her to return to the Captain and the children, telling her that God's walls were not made for running away from problems. Maria reluctantly returns.

Maria's absence was all that the Captain needed to make him realize his own love for her. He breaks his engagement to the Baroness and proposes to Maria.

After a lovely wedding, a storybook ending seems imminent, until the Nazi movement gains momentum in Austria, and Captain Von Trapp is "requested" to join the group. Always reluctant to let his family sing in public, he relents when their appearance in public becomes part of a scheme for the family to flee the country to escape the ugly political powers that are taking over. The family manages to escape from their escorts, and they take refuge in the abbey. In the film's final scene, they climb over the hills to cross the border and start a new life outside their beloved homeland.

For a list of musical numbers, see the Discography section **(D17)**.

Commentary

When *The Sound of Music* was unleashed on an unsuspecting public in 1965, no one -- least of all 20th-Century Fox -- was prepared for the phenomenal whirlwind of applause and boxoffice fireworks that was to greet it worldwide. It seemed nobody liked the film but the public. National critics tripped over each others thesauruses searching for new adjectives to replace *saccharine* and *sappy*. Meanwhile audiences lined up around the block in every city where the film played, going back to see it again and again -- and this was even before it shifted from hardticket to regular prices. In less than a year, the film surpassed *Gone With the Wind* as Hollywood's biggest boxoffice success up to that time.

What accounted for the euphoric, explosive audience acceptance? Everyone has their theories, of course, but in my book, two overriding factors cancel out all others: 1) It was an expertly crafted film entertainment selling pure Hollywood escapism at a time when audiences were sensing that romanticism in the movies was an endangered species; and 2) Julie's incandescent performance, pure and simple.

The Sound of Music, the last Rodgers and Hammerstein stage musical, was considered by many to be their weakest effort. This was in no small part due to a genuinely sappy, formulaic, and insipid book. It was turn-of-the-century style Bavarian operetta appearing in the Broadway era of the more realistic and dramatic *Gypsy* and *West Side Story*.

Although the critics complained of too much schmaltz, the most remarkable thing about director Robert Wise's film rendition was the way he *cut down* on the cutesyness of the material -- keeping the sweetness to a minimum. I can think of only one other example of a film musical that so miraculously and completely improved upon its stage version -- and that was 1972's *Cabaret*. For that effort, however, Bob Fossee made some rather radical changes in the source material. In *Music*, Wise stuck close to the original book and music, but somehow shifted the emphasis from a never-never-land fairy tale village to a sumptuously beautiful -- but realistic -- Nazi-era Austria.

He used many resources to accomplish that feat -- everything from breathtaking cinematography to expert editing. But his strongest ally in making *Music* more playable -- and believable -- was Julie Andrews.

Her freshness, warmth, sincerity, and completely relaxed screen presence allowed her to play against the frivolous nun/cheery nanny that the script called for. Her transition was more from a tomboyish girl into a full-fledged, beautiful woman. If the dialogue was sometimes sugar-coated, the performance was real enough to tip the balance in her favor. Here was a central character you could really believe in.

Probably because she played a governess in both this and *Poppins*, people frequently lump the two roles together when they want to deride Julie and classify her as a saccharine type. But in reality, the roles in *Poppins* and *Music* were quite different. In *Poppins*, she seemed appropriately ageless as she stylized the role to suit the musical fantasy genre that she was playing. In *Music*, she played a real person with real emotions, growing from girlhood to adulthood within the course of the story. She seemed to perfectly understand Wise's slant on the material, achieving believability through a genuinely warm, sincere approach to counteract the more manipulative bromides inherited from the play. The result was clearly a bravura star performance from a star whose career was skyrocketing into the stratosphere. Even most of those who didn't care for the film had words of praise for its glittering star.

Reviews

Variety (3/3/65) -- This trade paper was one of the few major media review sources to give *Music* a thorough endorsement, calling the film "one of the top musicals to reach the screen." The film was also called "a warmly pulsating, captivating drama set to the most imaginative use of the lilting Rodgers and Hammerstein tunes." Both the lavish production values and the cast got high marks from *Variety*. Julie was said to give her role "a sense of balance which assures continued star stature." Christopher Plummer was called "forceful." Eleanor Parker was said to "acquit herself with style." The musical numbers were said to be "expertly staged."

New York Times (3/3/65) -- The *Times* review was more typical of most major reviews, with its condescending tone. The film was said to "come close to being a careful duplication" of the stage version, "even down to its operetta pattern, which predates the cinema age." Julie was said to provide "the most apparent and fetching innovation in the film." The review claimed that she brought "a nice sort of Mary Poppins logic and authority" to the role of Maria. However, the reviewer felt that this role was constantly in danger of "collapsing under...romantic nonsense and sentiment." It was implied that Julie knew she was in a silly film, but went about her duties "happily and bravely." She allegedly played "a more saccharine nanny than Mary Poppins." The children were praised as doing the best they could with "assortedly artificial roles." The adult performers, however, were called "horrendous," with Christopher Plummer singled out among them.

*****

F04　　　*TORN CURTAIN*
　　　　　　(Universal; 1966; 128 minutes; Video: MCA)

Credits

Producer/Director	Alfred Hitchcock
Screenplay	Brian Moore
Camera (Technicolor)	John F. Warren
Editor	Bud Hoffman
Music	John Addison
Assistant Director	Donald Raer

Cast

Prof. Michael Armstrong	Paul Newman
Sarah Sherman	Julie Andrews
Countess Kuchinska	Lila Kedrova
Heinrich Gerhard	Hansjoerg Felmy
Ballerina	Tamara Toumanova
Hermann Gromek	Wolfgang Kieling
Prof. Karl Manfred	Gunter Strack
Prof. Gustav Lindt	Ludwig Donath
Mr. Jacobi	David Opatoshu
Dr. Koska	Gisela Fischer
Farmer	Mort Mills
Farmer's Wife	Carolyn Conwell
Freddy	Arthur Gould-Porter
Fraulein Mann	Gloria Gorvin
Hotel Travel Clerk	Erik Holland
Airlines Official	Hedley Mattingly
Gutman	Norbert Schiller
Olaf Hengstrom	Peter Bourne
Jacobi	Charles Radilack

Taxi Driver   Peter Lorr
Factory Manager   Frank Aberschal

Synopsis

Professor Michael Armstrong, a nuclear physicist, is attending a convention in Denmark, along with his secretary/fiancee Sarah Sherman. When he receives a message at his hotel to pick up a book that he had ordered at a local bookstore, he sends Sarah to get it for him. After Sarah presents the book to him, he looks inside for a secret message that has been planted for him. Then he tells Sarah that he must go to Copenhagen on sudden business. She wants to go along and can't understand it when he insists that she stay behind.

Curious about his mysterious behavior, she investigates at the hotel and discovers that his plane ticket is not for Copenhagen at all. He's headed for the Communist city of East Berlin. Wondering why he lied to her and what he could be doing behind the Iron Curtain, she buys a ticket for herself and, much to Michael's surprise, meets him on the plane.

Michael is angry at first, but once they arrive, realizes there's not much he can do. What Sarah doesn't know at first is that Michael is leading the Communists to believe that he is defecting to their side so that he can withdraw secret information about Russian missile projects from a famous German scientist, Ludwig Donath.

Before long, Sarah learns of Michael's true mission. Unfortunately, she isn't the only one. Michael struggles with and eventually kills a Communist guard who has followed him to a rendevouz with a secret agent at a local farmhouse. It isn't long before the Communists are suspicious.

Michael manages to trick Donath out of the information he was seeking, just before Communist agents begin to close in on him and Sarah. The chase is on.

An eccentric Polish refugee, Countess Kuchinska, agrees to help the two escape if they can secure a U.S. visa for her in exchange. While dodging their pursuers, Michael and Sarah take refuge in a theatre where a ballet performance is in progress. It soon becomes obvious that police are everywhere in the theatre. In desperation, Michael yells "Fire!" to cause a diversion. With the help of a CIA agent, Michael and Sarah hide in costume baskets and prepare to stow away on a ship to Sweden.

As the ship is ready to depart, the police come aboard and demand to inspect the two clothes baskets, presuming that the American spies are inside. When they meet with resistance, they open fire on the baskets, which, it turns out, contain nothing but clothes. In another section of the ship, Michael and Sarah jump overboard and swim to safety in Stockholm.

Commentary

Torn Curtain, Alfred Hitchcok's 50th film, was greeted with high expectations when it premiered in summer, 1966. Julie, Hollywood's hottest female star at the time was teamed with perennial superstar Paul Newman in a new thriller from the master of screen suspense.

Hitchcock had directed some of the screen's most glamorous female stars (including Janet Leigh, Doris Day, Kim Novak, Grace Kelly) in what are now considered classic films (*Psycho, The Man Who Knew Too Much*, *Vertigo*, and *Rear Window*, respectively). Certainly, Julie's fans were expecting lighting to strike again.

Unfortunately, the bolt of lightning was more like a tiny spark. Like most of Hitchcock's last few films, *Torn Curtain* was lackluster and mostly unexciting. Nowhere was there a single moment to rival such classic Hitchcock scenes as the infamous shower sequence in *Psycho*, the Mt. Rushmore chase in *North by Northwest*, or the clash of cymbals in *The Man Who Knew Too Much*. Movie fans would have never recognized this as a Hitchcock film without being told that it was.

Even with the star power of Andrews and Newman, the film looked and played like a TV Movie-of-the-Week. It was not a terrible or shameful effort, but it was certainly no more than mediocre. Considering the talents involved, it was a major disappointment.

This was the first film in which Julie was expected to leave *Mary Poppins* back in Edwardian England forever. Her semi-nude bedroom scene with Paul Newman was the obligatory sort of slightly titillating scene that appeared in most films at the time. Though highly publicized, it was as tepid and dull as everything else in the picture, and had no impact.

All in all, this was not Julie's most shining hour in the cinema.

Reviews
Variety (7/20/66) -- The lukewarm *Variety* reaction to this film ("an okay Cold War suspenser") was more favorable than most reviews. The reviewer felt that Hitchcock's film recalled some of his earlier work, particularly in his suspense and "ironic comedy flair." Some scenes were called "intriguing," but the plot was said to be hampered by "routine dialogue." The reviewer further complained of a leisurely pace, asserting that early telegraphing of information diminished suspense. Newman was said to offer a "good underplaying to his role." Julie's "charming voice and appearance" were send to "lend grace to a limited but billed-over-title role."

New York Times (7/28/66) -- This review ("a pathetically undistinguished spy picture") was closer to the majority opinion than *Variety's*. Hitchcock was said to be hampered by "a blah script." The film's hero and heroine were accused of missing the point. The film was said to lack "surprises, suspense, or fun." Julie was compared to "an English nanny who means to see that no harm comes to [Newman]."

*****

F05   *HAWAII*
             (United Artists; 1966; 171 minutes; Video: CBS/Fox)

Credits
Based on the novel by James A. Michener

Director	George Roy Hill
Producer	Walter Mirisch
Associate Producer	Lewis J. Rachmil
Screenplay	Dalton Trumbo
	Daniel Taradash
Camera (DeLuxe)	Russell Harlan
Second Unit Camera	Howard Wellman
Prolog Camera	Chuck Wheeler
Editor	Stuart Gilmore
Music	Elmer Bernstein
Song: "My Wishing Doll"	Elmer Bernstein (music)
	Mack David (lyrics)
Production Design	Cary Odell
Assistant Director	Ray Gosnell
Second Unit Director	Richard Talmadge
Prolog Supervisor	James Blue

Cast

Jerusa Bromley	Julie Andrews
Abner Hale	Max Von Sydow
Rafer Foxworth	Richard Harris

Charles	Carroll O'Connor
Abigail	Elizabeth Cole
Charity	Diane Sherry
Mercy	Heather Menzies
Rev. Thorn	Torin Thatcher
John Whipple	Gene Hackman
Immanuel Qigley	John Cullum
Abraham Hewlett	Lou Antonio
Queen Malama	Jocelyn LeGarde
Keoki	Manu Tupou
Kelolo	Ted Nobriga
Nolelani	Elizabeth Logue
Iliki	Lokelani S. Chicarell
Gideon	Malcolm Atterbury
Hepzibah	Dorothy Jeakins
Captain Janders	George Rose
Mason	Michael Constantine
Collins	John Harding
Cridland	Robert Crawford
Micah at 4	Robert Oakley
Micah at 7	Henrik Von Sydow
Micah at 12	Clas S. Von Sydow
Micah at 18	Bertil Werjefelt
Passenger	Bette Midler

Synopsis

The story begins in 1820 in New England's Protestant community, where missionaries are planning to travel to the Hawaiian islands to convert the natives to Christianity.

Abner Hale is a by-the-book religious fundamentalist who is anxious to make the journey to spread God's word to the heathens, but must have a wife to accompany him. He is introduced to a pretty young maiden, Jerusa Bromley, who has been pining away for a sea captain she hasn't seen in years who has stopped corresponding with her. She decides to accept the marriage proposal offered by Abner.

The missionary group, including Abner and his new wife, set sail for the Islands. They suffer a turbulent, difficult journey through storm-tossed Cape Horn, but eventually reach their destination.

They meet the kindly native queen Malama, who takes an instant liking to the charming Jerusa. It is more difficult to warm up to the Puritanical Abner, who instantly takes issue with the native customs and rituals and vehemently pontificates fire-and-brimstone. Although some of the native practices (which include incest and the murdering of deformed infants) would be offensive to even non-Christians, Hale is too pompous and abrupt with his pressures for instant reform. Jerusa has a better understanding of basic human compassion, realizing that you can't change the lifelong beliefs of a people overnight and you needn't attack all aspects of their culture if you wish to gain their trust. Abner's hell-and-damnation approach leaves no room for such a quality as patience.

Despite the severity of Abner's approach, Malama supports and promotes his beliefs. This is a genuine sacrifice for her, since she and her brother, Nobriga, have been living as husband and wife.

Abner's objectives suffer a setback when a group of lusty sailors arrive on the island, seducing the native girls. Abner forbids the girls to mingle with the sailors, and the sailors retaliate be setting fire to Abner's chapel. The blaze is contained before extensive damage occurs. Worse yet for Abner, Jerusa's long-lost sea captain, Rafer Hoxworth, is among the group of sailors. Jerusa is momentarily tempted to follow her passions, but ultimately reaffirms her commitment to Hale.

The natives face more loss of identity and culture, as more Americans and sailors begin to come to the islands, bringing with them crass commercialism and new diseases. Epidemics of measles and other ailments spread. Unaccustomed to the diseases, the natives panic and sometimes worsen their condition by trying to cool their fever by running into the ocean. Malama falls ill and dies, but is baptized by Abner before she expires.

In the ensuing years, Abner continues to pontificate and strictly discipline the natives, while Jerusa makes futile efforts to convince him to have more compassion. Three sons are born to Abner and Jerusa.

Several years later, Rafer returns to the island and discovers that Jerusa is dead. He takes out his anger by beating on Abner, who will not lift a finger to defend himself. Eventually Abner is asked to retire, to be replaced in his post by a new minister. He sends his sons off to school in England, but decides to stay on in Hawaii. He feels that God expects him to live the rest of his life helping to teach the heathens.

Commentary

This is arguably the best of Julie's nonmusical films to date. Those who expressed surprise in 1986 at her moving dramatic performances in *That's Life!* and *Duet For One* must never have seen *Hawaii*. (Or they somehow blocked it out of their memory when the media's anti-Julie campaign of the 70s gained momentum.)

In this sprawling, historical epic, Julie came across as magnificently beautiful, moving, and very believable in every aspect of her role. She held her own against the more ostentatious Max von Sydow role and the scene-stealing bravura of Jocelyn LeGarde.

The film was beautifully made and generally engrossing, although the one-note religious fanaticism of its chief protagonist, Abner Hale, was tiresome and hardly condusive to audience empathy. Julie helped to balance this out somewhat with her usual pleasing screen presence. She was quite believable in the role of a well-bred and compassionate woman who believed in God but did not need to carry her belief to the destructive extremes that her husband did.

Although she played a woman of kindness, character, and breeding, the role was not the goody-goody stereotype she has often been accused of playing. The character of Jerusha is too full-bodied to be dismissed in such a way. In fact, her lack of religious fanaticism is refreshing in this context, because it makes her more human. She obviously had respect for her faith and the New England Protestant ethics, but she was smart enough to know that people should not be expected to be perfect.

The film was a prestigious big-budget epic on a scale seldom attempted nowadays. It did not receive a strong enough reception to put in the classic stature of a *Lawrence of Arabia* or an *Exodus*. But it was a credit that Julie can be proud of, and demonstrates that from the earliest part of her career, she did not want to be cast in a *Mary Poppins* mold.

Reviews

Variety (10/5/66) -- At the head of the group of those cheering this film on, the industry's main trade paper called the film "excellent." Production values, the script (based on a portion of James Michener's mammoth novel), and the acting were all termed "topknotch." Max Von Sydow was said to be "terrific" in the Abner Hale role. Julie was called "excellent in a demanding dramatic role." The supporting ensemble cast also drew praise ("uniformly strong performances"). Technical credits were called "first rate."

New York Times (10/11/66) -- Much harsher than *Variety* on the film, the *Times* was "not so much moved as numbed" by the film's overwhelming scenes of turbulent seas, violent storms, and "pomp and pestilence." Though the film was said to superficially adhere to "the episodic shape and gaudy surface of a conventional romantic spectacle," the reviewer took issue with the film's protagonist, Rev. Abner Hale. The reviewer saw this character as "a rigid, narrow-minded, sometimes ridiculous man of God." Although Von Sydow was said to give a good performance, the reviewer found such a character inappropriate for this film. "Not since the Rev. Mr. Davidson went after Sadie Thompson," said the reviewer, " has Protestant Christian proselytism come off so poorly on the screen." Von Sydow and Julie, according to the reviewer, "contributed the film's few moments of genuine emotion."

*****

F06 **THOROUGHLY MODERN MILLIE**
(Universal; 1967; 138 minutes; Video: MCA)

Credits

Director	George Roy Hill
Producer	Ross Hunter
Screenplay	Richard Morris
New Songs	Sammy Cahn
	Jimmy Van Heusen
Score	Elmer Bernstein
Score Adaptation	Andre Previn
	Joseph Gershenson
Camera (Technicolor)	Russell Metty
Choreography	Joe Layton
Editor	Stu Gilmore

Cast

Millie Dillmount	Julie Andrews
Dorothy Brown	Mary Tyler Moore
Muzzy Van Hossmere	Carol Channing
Jimmy Smith	James Fox
Trevor Graydon	John Gavin
Mrs. Meers	Beatrice Lillie
Number One	Jack Soo
Number Two	Pat Morita
Tea	Philip Ahn
Miss Flannery	Cavada Humphrey
Juarez	Anthony Dexter
Cruncher	Lou Nova
Baron Richter	Michael St. Clair
Adrian	Albert Carrier
Gregory Huntley	Victor Rogers
Judith Tremaine	Lizabeth Hush
Taxi Driver	Herbie Faye
Singer	Ann Dee
Waiter	Benny Rubin
Dorothy's dance partner	Buddy Schwab
Pianist	Jay Thompson
Male Pedestrian	Todd Mason
Woman in Office	Mae Clarke

Synopsis

Millie Dillmount is a young girl in 1920s New York who is determined to be a "modern" -- which means dressing provocatively, keeping up with the latest fads, and marrying her rich boss (when she finds one). She lives at the women's boarding house of Mrs. Meers, unaware that the hotel is a front for Meers and her Oriental henchmen to kidnap young orphan girls and whisk them off for sale to a white slave ring. ("Sad to be all alone in the world," is Mrs. Meer's ironic refrain.)

Millie befriends the wealthy but oh-so-pure Miss Dorothy, the eccentric millionairess Muzzy, and the effervescent -- but penniless -- Jimmy. She lands a job as secretary to a handsome insurance executive, and sets out to snare him for a husband. Unfortunately, he has eyes only for Miss Dorothy.

Meanwhile, Millie shuns the person who is truly in love with her -- the ever-patient Jimmy. "Follow your heart," Muzzy advises Millie, but Millie's dreams of marrying a millionaire don't leave room for something as frivolous as romance.

The film reaches its climax when Mrs. Meers finally succeeds in kidnapping Miss Dorothy. Millie and her pals set out for Chinatown to rescue her, and a mad chase ensues.

A "surprise" ending (actually pretty predictable if you know your 20's melodramas) eventually sets things right for everyone. Suffice it to say that Muzzy's advice to Millie was sound.

For a list of musical numbers, see the Discography section (**D22**).

Commentary

Julie was at the peak of her popularity when this lavish musical premiered. No one could have predicted that this would be Julie's last commercially successful musical until *Victor/Victoria* in 1982.

Despite its boxoffice success, however, *Millie* remains one of Julie's most problematical films. Its appeal depends on overlooking its belabored second half, after a terrifically entertaining beginning.

In the mid-60s, the trend in films was towards big-budget 3-hour extravaganzas. These films -- everything from musicals to historical epics -- were called "roadshow attractions," meaning they opened at inflated ticket prices in metropolitan areas, then gradually made their way to the hinterlands after an anticipation factor (hopefully) had developed. This trend hurt many films that begged for a simpler, less pretentious treatment. *Thoroughly Modern Millie* was one of them.

Producer Ross Hunter had been frustrated in his unsuccessful attempts to secure the film rights to Julie's first Broadway stage hit, the flapper musical, *The Boy Friend*. (It was eventually made by Ken Russell in 1971 with Twiggy in Julie's role.) As a compromise, Hunter finally decided to put together a Roaring 20s musical of his own.

Besides Julie, he signed up two impressive costars for supporting roles: Carol Channing (fresh off her *Hello, Dolly!* stage triumph) as an eccentric millionairess and 30s comedienne Beatrice Lillie as a diabolical Oriental hotel manager. A pre-Mary-Richards Mary Tyler Moore rounded out the female cast as Millie's saccharine-sweet ingenue pal, Miss Dorothy. John Gavin and James Fox took the romantic male leads.

The casting and the lively musical score gave the film its initial burst of energy. (The score combined new ditties by Sammy Cahn and Jimmy Van Heusen with standard songs of the 20s.) Added to this, the typically sumptuous Ross Hunter trappings (pastel Technicolor sets, authentic period costumes and cars, stylish cinematography) and the spritely direction of George Roy Hill (who had previously directed Julie in *Hawaii*) got the film off to a rousing start.

The post-intermission stretch was another story. The slapstick became more heavyhanded, the sight gags more preposterous, the frenetic chases more tiresome, as the film went on. What started as a witty 20s satire gradually declined into a routine chase adventure.

Nevertheless, Julie was a delight throughout. She obviously relished a role that was not dripping with spoonfulls-of-sugar or Bavarian strudel. As she brazenly raised her skirtline, abandoned her girlish curls, and set out to vamp her handsome boss, she showed more comic versatility than in her previous roles. Inspired by the zany material, her comic timing was sharper than ever before, and her star power was bright enough to dominate the proceedings, despite hefty competition from the antics of seasoned pros Channing and Lillie.

The film is remembered by more moviegoers than *Star!* (1968) or *Darling Lili* (1970), which were more ambitious musicals that failed to catch on.

Reviews

Variety (3/23/67) -- The industry's major trade paper responded favorably, if unexcitedly, to the film. Like many other reviewers, *Variety* complained about the laborious post-intermission doldrums that dragged the film down. However, the reviewer felt that Julie was an advantage to the film's enjoyment, with Carol Channing "perhaps [an] even greater advantage." Calling the overall effort "an uneven comedy," the paper's boxoffice prognosis was "it will probably do ok."

New York Times (3/23/67) -- The *Times* was much more enthusiastic than *Variety* about the film ("a thoroughly delightful movie"). The reviewer especially liked Julie, Carol Channing, and Beatrice Lillie, who were said to be "working hard to see which can be the most delightfully extravagant, galvanic, and droll." Julie was termed "absolutely darling...deliciously spirited and dry." Like other reviewers, the *Times* complained of the "phony and gratuitous" Jewish wedding scene" and the second half's "melodramatic mishmash."

*****

F07   ***THE SINGING PRINCESS***
(Larry Joachim Productions; 1967; 66 minutes; Video: Goodtimes)

Animated children's movie featuring Julie's voice. See Appendix B for more information.

*****

F08   ***STAR!***
(20th Century-Fox; 1968; 165 minutes; Video: None)

Credits

Director	Robert Wise
Producer	Saul Chaplin
Screenplay	William Fairchild
Title Song	Sammy Cahn
	James Van Husen
Orchestration	Lennie Hayton
Camera (DeLuxe)	Ernest Laszlo
Dance/musical numbers (staging)	Michael Kidd

Production design	Boris Leven
Costumes	Donald Brooks
Editor	William Reynolds
Sound	Murray Spivack
	Douglas Williams
	Bernard Freericks
Sets	Walter M. Scott
	Howard Bristol
Special Effects	L. B. Abbott
	Art Cruickshank
Dance Assistant	Shelah Hackett

Additional songs, music, and material by Saul Chaplin, Walter Williams, Bruce Siever, Paul Morande, J. P. Long, Maurice Scott, Noel Coward, Bud deSylva, Gus Kahn, Al Jolson, William Hargreaves, Philip Braham, Douglas Furber, Ira and George Gershwin, Cole Porter, Kurt Weill.

Cast

Gertrude Lawrence	Julie Andrews
Richard Aldrich	Richard Crenna
Sir Anthony Spencer	Michael Craig
Noel Coward	Daniel Massey
Charles Fraser	Robert Reed
Arthur Lawrence	Bruce Forsyth
Rose	Beryl Reid
Jack Roper	John Collin
Andre Charlot	Alan Openheimer
David Holtzman	Richard Karlan
Billie Carleton	Lynley Lawrence
Jack Buchanan	Garrett Lewis
Jeannie Banks	Elizabeth St. Clair
Pamela	Jenny Agutter
Ben Mitchell	Anthony Eisley
Alexander Woollcott	Jock Livingston
Dan	J. Pat O'Malley
Lord Chamberlain	Lester Matthews
Assistant to Lord Chamberlain	Bernard Fox
Bankruptcy Judge	Murray Matheson
Hyde Park Speaker	Robin Hughes
Daffodil Girls	Jeannette Landis
	Dinah Ann Rogers
	Barbara Sandland
	Ellen Plasschaert
	Ann Hubbell

Synopsis

The film begins with an overture of the songs to follow, performed as if we were in a live theatre watching an orchestra (the same opening gimmick, incidentally, used in the 1963 film *Gypsy* and modified for *A Little Night Music* in 1978). The overture segues into a small-screen black-and-white documentary called *Star!*, composed of old-looking newsreel footage. We appear to be watching a 40s-produced documentary of the early life of Gertrude Lawrence, circa 1915.

Suddenly, we switch to widescreen color as a middle-aged Gertie (circa 1940) yells out to stop the projector. We realize that the documentary we've been watching is a film-within-a-film, as an adult Gertie sits in a screening room, viewing a chronological film about the events of her life and career. Before long, we are back to the black-and-white documentary again. But the documentary soon gives way to a full-color version of the story. The documentary format is only returned to occasionally throughout the rest of the film.

The story follows Gertie's life, beginning at age 16, as she performed with her father in tacky British musical halls, and ending with her New York stage performance in Kurt Weill's *Lady in the Dark* in 1941. The film ends several years before her death at age 54 in 1952.

Such real-life celebrities as Noel Coward (played by Daniel Massey) are involved in the proceedings, which essentially center around Lawrence's romantic flirtations, unhappy marriages, extravagance, egocentric behavior, and drunken bouts.

The action is frequently interrupted for production numbers ranging from such early vaudeville turns as "Burlington Bertie From Bow" to 30s and 40s musical comedy standards by Cole Porter, George and Ira Gerswhwin, Noel Coward, and Kurt Weill. The film ends on an upbeat note with Lawrence's marriage to wealthy banker Richard Aldrich (played by Richard Crenna) in 1941.

For a list of musical numbers, see the Discography section **(D23)**.

Commentary

When I began researching *Star!*, two very interesting facts about the film came to light: (1) in general, the reviews weren't nearly as bad as memory seemed to recall; (2) it seems more entertaining now than it did in its initial release. Perhaps we overlook the flaws because we are starved for the kind of big-scale musical extravaganza that *Star!* represents -- essentially a relic nowadays. Or perhaps we were brainwashed at the time by all of the anti-Julie sentiments that dominated the press for years after the financial failures of both *Star!* and *Darling Lili* (1970).

If you approach *Star!* more from the standpoint of a Julie Andrews vehicle than a Gertrude Lawrence biography, you'll find much less to quibble about. Most moviegoers are not too familiar with Lawrence, the British stage star. Most who knew Lawrence or her work felt that neither the script nor Julie's performance captured the essence of Lawrence's sultry temperament or a meaningful commentary on her life. Those who didn't know Lawrence didn't care, of course, as long as the film was entertaining.

Curiously, the film ends abruptly in 1941, nine years before Gertrude Lawrence's death. It would have been interesting to see Julie play scenes from the roles Lawrence was best known for in the U.S., which mostly happened after 1941. This included costarring on Broadway with Yul Brynner in Rodgers and Hammerstein's *The King and I*, the film version of Tennessee Williams' *The Glass Menagerie*, and Eliza Doolittle in *Pygmalion*. Since Julie played the role of Eliza in the musical *My Fair Lady*, wouldn't some *Pygmalion* scenes have been fascinating?

Perhaps Wise wanted to avoid the unhappy aspects of Lawrence's later years. (Did the sugar-and-spice influence of *The Sound of Music*'s memory win out?) Or perhaps the intent was to limit the scope of the story to allow time for the music. In any case, the omissions seem like missed opportunities.

Part of the letdown of the film was surely due to its pedigree. Director Robert Wise reassembled most of the creative talent behind *The Sound of Music* (1965), Julie's most resounding success. The film was soundly criticized for not being another *Sound of Music* (although it never really tried to be).

Star! was a more sophisticated film than *Music* -- both in subject matter and in execution. More a dramatic film with music than a musical, *Star!* confined its musical numbers to on-stage performances, rather than the singing-in-the-rain type of musical convention that was already becoming passe in 1968.

From a budgetary and logistical standpoint, *Star!* was no less ambitious than *Music*. Julie sported dozens of sumptuous Donald Brooks gowns and appeared in some 15 lavishly staged musical numbers. No holds were barred in mounting a first-class film, and the result was six Academy nominations in the technical categories.

After disastrous opening engagements as a roadshow attraction, the film was pulled out of release, shortened by 50 minutes, retitled *Those Were the Happy Days*, and re-released to an even more apathetic boxoffice response than before. Ever since that time, the film has appeared occasionally in revival houses and on television (titled *Star!* again), edited to various lengths, but still remaining obscure to the memory of most moviegoers.

Nevertheless, at a West Hollywood revival house screening of the film's complete three-hour roadshow version in 1983, the audience was apparently full of Andrews fans, who thunderously applauded each musical number, buzzed enthusiastically at intermission, and generally approached the afternoon as if it were a cinematic event equivalent to the second coming of *Citizen Kane*. When I asked the film's producer Saul Chaplin (who attended the screening) whether he thought Hollywood would ever again make the kind of glamorous, lavish musical extravaganza that *Star!* represents, he wistfully replied, "I certainly hope so." As of this writing, his hope remains unfulfilled.

Reviews

Variety (7/23/68) -- *Variety* felt that *Star!* suffered from problems that were typical of films released in a roadshow fashion: "it's overlong... and occasionally sags between musical numbers." However, the reviewer liked the "witty and knowledgeable" original script by William Fairchild. The film was seen as "a pleasing tribute" to its real-life protagonist, Gertrude Lawrence. The role of Lawrence was said to be a "tricky but meaty" one for Julie, who delivered "a carefully built-up performance." The paper felt that the film would be enjoyable for fans of Julie Andrews and Lawrence alike.

New York Times (10/23/68) -- The most telling point about the *Times* review was its sheer brevity (250 words), which in itself could be read as a major insult for such a big-budgeted, eagerly awaited production. The reviewer found Julie "not at her best." The songs were said to come across as "mechanical and cold." The paper suggested that devotees of old-fashioned musicals might enjoy it, but that Gertrude Lawrence fans would be disappointed.

*****

F09   *DARLING LILI*
            (Paramount; 1970; 139 minutes; Video: None)

Credits

Producer/Director	Blake Edwards
Executive Producer	Owen Crump
Associate Producer	Ken Wales
Screenplay	Blake Edwards
	William Peter Blatty
Music	Henry Mancini
Lyrics	Johnny Mercer
Camera (Technicolor)	Russell Harlan
Choreography	Hermes Pan
Production Design	Fernando Carriere
Assistant Directors	Mickey McCardle
	Gene Marum
Costumes	Donald Brooks
	Jack Bear
Editor	Peter Zinner
Special Effects	Bob Peterson

Cast

Lili Smith	Julie Andrews
Maj. William Larrabee	Rock Hudson
Kurt von Ruger	Jeremy Kemp
Lt. Carstairs Twombley-Crouch	Lance Percival
Major Duvalle	Jacques Marin
Lt. George Youngblood Carson	Michael Witney
Lt. Liggett	Andre Maranne
Bedford	Bernard Kay
Emma	Doreen Keogh
Suzette	Gloria Paul
Kessler	Carl Deuring
Kraus	Vernon Dobtchell
Sgt. Wells	A. E. Gould-Porter
French Generals	Louis Mercer
	Laurie Main
Baron von Richthofen	Ingo Mogendorf
Von Hindenburg	Niall MacGinnis
Chanteuse	Mimi Monti

Synopsis

During World War I, Lili Smith is a British stage star who is also a spy for Germany, assigned to draw war secrets out of Allied officers. Lili reports to Von Ruger, a German Intelligence colonel who pretends to be her uncle from Switzerland.

Her latest assignment, in France, is to extract secret information about military aircraft manuevers from Major William Larrabee, the handsome ace commander of the Eagle Squadron, who engages in aerial dogfight warfare against the German forces, most notably the notorious Red Baron. Lili's mission is to use her feminine wiles to seduce Larrabee, then to pry the desired information out of him.

At first, the gambit appears to be working without a hitch, as Lili begins dating Larrabee, quickly gaining his trust and affection. However, she is soon visited by two bungling French Intelligence detectives, Major Duvalle and Lieutenant Liggett. They have approached Lili because she has been seen publicly with Larrabee. The officers inform Lili that they have reason to suspect that Major Larrabee is passing valuable military secrets to a female German secret agent. Lili feigns astonishment, and promises to cooperate with the men by letting them know if she detects anything that may help them confirm their beliefs.

When the agents leave, Lili explains her dilemma to Von Ruger: Since the French Intelligence has obviously picked up some clues, they will eventually figure out that she is the spy if she continues to see Larrabee. On the other hand, if she stops seeing Larrabee and the flow of information comes to an abrupt halt, the Intelligence office will know immediately that she is the spy. It appears to be a no-win situation. To complicate matters further, Lili is clearly falling in love with Larrabee, a situation that cannot help but confuse her loyalties and her sense of rational judgement.

When Larrabee's flying partner, Lieutenant Trombley-Crouch, accidentally mentions "Operations Crepe Suzette" in front of her, Lili assumes that she has stumbled upon the code name for a major Allied military offensive and reports this to Von Ruger. After Von Ruger investigates this, he informs Lili that there is no evidence of such a plan in the works.

The two bungling French detectives soon have they answer. It seems that Operation Crepe Suzette actually refers to a voluptuos Parisan stripper named Suzette who is romantically involved with Larrabee. Assuming that Suzette is the spy they have been looking for, the detectives come to Lili with their discovery.

After Lili goes to see the sexy Suzette perform her act, she flies into a jealous rage. It's clear by this point that Lili's emotions will cancel out any questions of loyalty to a particular country. In a foolish ploy to get back at Suzette, Lili plants false evidence in Suzette's room, then tips off the French Intelligence to search there.

As a result, Suzette and Larrabee face treason charges. In spite of their innocence, Larrabee's value to the German Intelligence as an unwitting information source is now destroyed because of the scrutiny he will be under. Worse yet, Lili's misplaced sense of justice in the frameup receives another jolt when Suzette publicly admits that Larrabee had informed her that he was breaking off his relationship with her because of his love for Lili Smith.

Feeling guilty and distraught, Lili takes off for the French Intelligence headquarters to make a full confession, hoping to clear Larrabee. Meanwhile, Von Ruger is visited by a German Intelligence officer who informs him that he will be escorted back to Germany, where he is to be courtmartialed for botching the Larrabee assignment. Lili is destined for an even worse fate: At that moment, she is being trailed by an assassin who has been instructed to gun her down for doublecrossing the Germans.

Managing to overpower and evade his escort, Von Ruger rushes to French Intelligence to warn Lili that an assassin is seeking her out. He arrives just as Lili is leaving the building and pushes her out of the range of fire in the nick of time. They speed away in a chauffeured car.

Von Ruger informs Lili that their only hope of escaping the German assassins is to flee to sanctuary in Switzerland via train. Lili realizes her love for Larrabee more than ever and is reluctant to leave.

Von Ruger points out to Lili that her confession has done nothing for Larrabee. If she stays in France and is convicted, the Major will still be tried for conspiracy. If she leaves the country and does not contact Larrabee for a good while, there's a much better chance that he will be cleared of any charges.

They board the train for Switzerland, and the escape appears to be going smoothly until the assassin enters their compartment and holds them at gunpoint. As it turns out, however, there's an even worse danger on the way. The Germans have decided to take an even bolder tactic. They have detached the Red Baron and his fleet to attack the train before it reaches the Swiss border.

When Larrabee learns about this, he boards his plane and sets out to rescue Lili. He arrives on the scene just as the attack has begun. He and the Baron battle it out, with Larrabee emerging victorious. In the midst of the attack, the assassin is killed. Lili and Von Ruger jump off the train and flee on foot, with Lili waving goodbye to Larrabee. They make it safely across the border.

Soon thereafter, the war is declared over. Lili has apparently resigned herself to her separation from Larrabee. Back in London, she is performing in a benefit concert for the war relief fund when Larrabee suddenly shows up onstage. The lovers are joyously reunited and Lili's adventurous days as a spy are now a mere memory.

For a list of musical numbers, see the Discography section (**D24**).

Commentary

Like *Star!*, *Darling Lili* is a better film than its reputation would lead us to believe. The first of many collaborations between Julie and her future (at that time) husband, producer/director Blake Edwards, the film is part World War I spy adventure, part musical comedy, part sex farce, with a little of everything else sort of thrown in. As with other Blake Edwards films, it's an odd blend of diverse styles and genres. But it's also an extravagant, glamorous entertainment -- the type of multimillion dollar fluffball that became increasingly rare in the realistic, hard-edged era of films in the 70s and 80s.

Julie as a Mata Hari type *femme fatale* spy teamed for the first time with Doris Day's pillow-talking partner Rock Hudson. The chemistry worked well, providing a warm and funny battle-of-the-sexes storyline to counterbalance the suspenseful moments and the spectacular aerial battle sequences.

Thanks to media hype, the film was widely publicized at the time for Julie and Hudson's sexy shower scene (toned down for the U. S. release version) and her first strip scene -- a comic burlesque number. This was the first of Edwards' ongoing attempts to prove to the world that his fair lady was more than a prim-and-proper

British nanny. It was followed more than a decade later by her breast-baring scene in *S.O.B.* (see **F14**) and her role as a mock homosexual female impersonator in *Victor/Victoria* (see **F15**).

Julie sang several new songs by Henry Mancini (music) and Johnny Mercer (lyrics), including the Oscar-nominated "Whistling in the Dark," plus "I'll Give You Three Guesses" (first done as a *Mary Poppins* - type number, then later as a strip tease), "Smile Away Each Rainy Day," and "The Girl in No Man's Land." In the opening sequence during the credits, she sang a medley of popular World War I songs, such as "Keep the Home Fires Burning", "It's a Long Way to Tipperary", and "Pack Up Your Troubles in an Old Kit Bag."

As in Star!, Julie's character was a singer, and all songs were integrated into the storyline. This more realistic approach was becoming the new trend for film musicals at the time, replacing the Broadway/operetta type of style.

Like other highly touted multimillion-dollar boxoffice blowouts (Cleopatra, Heaven's Gate, Ishtar), Darling Lili is a film that seems to be destined for a place in film history more for its legendary budget overruns and monumental production problems than for an unbiased artistic appraisal. The advance publicity was so bad that most critics were poised for the kill long before the film opened. Predictably, they spared no arsenal, attacking the harmless marshmallow of a film as if it were a major Communist invasion of the country. This was the beginning of a long let's-get-Julie media campaign that was to hamper Julie's career and peace of mind for years to come.

At the time, Arthur Knight commented (see **B36**) that with the recesssion that existed in Hollywood that year, one would think that everyone in the industry would be praying for a hit -- which would help the industry at large. But talks of film success are not as good for cocktail party conversation as impending disaster. Knight commented that several Hollywood naysayers who had been prepared to hate Lili were shocked to find that they actually enjoyed it.

Blake Edwards was so bitter about the backlash on the film -- his fights with the Paramount brass and the cruel media barbs -- that the vitrol he stored up eventually spewed forth in 1981, in *S.O.B.* (see **F14**), his scathing satire of the Hollywood filmmaking community (ironically, also released by Paramount).

Judged on its own terms, *Darling Lili* is an entertaining, if overstuffed, bon-bon of a film that was a good showcase for Julie's comedic and singing talents. It was a financial failure (to put it mildly), but there were some highly favorable reviews scattered among the critical brickbats. The *New York Times* even found it an interesting enough film to review twice. In recent years, it has achieved somewhat of a cult following, although it curiously remains unavailable on home video.

Reviews

Variety (7/22/70) -- In its usual dollars-and-cents review slant, *Variety* clearly misjudged this film by calling it "a generally strong boxoffice attraction." However, the paper also had its misgivings, not quite comprehending how the pieces of the film were supposed to fit together ("this is supposed to be a comedy -- or is it?") Julie's farcical striptease routine was called " a...highlight." However, Julie's character was seen as "too contrived." She was said to be at her best when singing.

New York Times (7/24/70) -- The *Times* liked the film much more than most other major reviewers, calling it "a pure if not perfect comedy." Its liabilities were seen to be that it was "big, long, overproduced," but on the plus side, the reviewer detected "a lot of perverse charm and real cinematic beauty." It was suggested that Julie was possibly "the perfect centerpiece for this sort of fantasy," with her angular and aggressive countenance humorously counterpointing her *femme fatale* character. Rock Hudson was said to offer "beautiful support" in the role of Major Larrabee.

*****

F10   *THE TAMARIND SEED*
(Avco Embassy; 1974; 123 minutes; Video: Embassy)

Credits

Based on the novel by Evelyn Anthony

Director/Screenplay	Blake Edwards
Producer	Ken Wales
Music	John Barry
Song: "Play it Again"	John Barry (music)
	John Black (lyrics)
Sung by	Wilma Reading
Camera (color)	Freddie Young
Associate Producer	Johnny Goodman
Art Director	Harry Pottle
Editor	Ernest Walter
Assistant Director	Derek Cracknell

Cast

Judith Farrow	Julie Andrews
Feodor Sverdlov	Omar Sharif
Jack Loder	Anthony Quayle
Fergus Stephenson	Daniel O'Herlihy
Margaret Stephenson	Sylvia Sims
General Golitsyn	Oscar Homolka
George MacLeod	Bryan Marshall
Richard Patterson	David Baron
Rachael Patterson	Celia Bannerman
Colonel Moreau	Roger Dann
Sandy Mitchell	Sharon Duce
Major Sukalov	George Mikell
Anna Skriabina	Kate O'Mara
Dimitiri Memenov	Constantin De Goguel
First KGB Agent	John Sullivan
Second KGB Agent	Terence Plummer
Third KGB Agent	Leslie Crawford
Igor Kalinin	Alexei Jawdokimov
Embassy Section Head	Janet Henfry

Synopsis

To get over a broken love affair with a married man, Judith Farrow a British civil servant, takes a vacation in Barbados. She meets a dashing Russian, Feodor Sverdlov. There is an immediate attraction, but Judith is reluctant to rush into a new romance, still smarting from her most recent ill-fated romantic involvement. Nevertheless, she continues to see him.

Since Judith is an assistant to a high-ranking British government official and Feodor is the Soviet air attache in Paris, both British and Russian Intelligence agencies are soon trailing the couple, both sides fearing they may be dealing with a traitor passing secrets to an enemy agent. Unbeknownst to Judith, Feodor has told his superiors that he hopes to enlist Judith as a spy for the Russians. But his motives are not clear -- to the Russians or to Judith.

As Moscow becomes more distrustful, Feodor is ordered to return home. Fearful of the fate that probably awaits him when he gets there, he decides to defect. Before he is allowed to defect, however, he must aid the British government by helping them get the goods on an important British official who is suspected of being a Russian spy.

A series of complications continues to challenge the budding romance, as uncertainty about each other's motives and pressures from their respective governments abound to cause the lovers difficulty at every level. Eventually, Feodor is presumed dead after the building he was last seen is explodes, obviously the victim of a political assassination.

A grief-stricken Judith returns to London to pick up the pieces after a second disastrous romance. Suddenly, Feodor turns up. He somehow escaped the burning building and no longer has any ties with the Russian government. The lovers are finally on the same side of the political fence.

Commentary

After an absence of four years, Julie returned to the screen with her second film for her director/husband Blake Edwards. It also happened to be her third espionage adventure (preceded by Hitchcock's *Torn Curtain* in 1966 and Edwards' *Darling Lili* in 1970).

Though beautifully mounted and well acted, this was probably the least involving of her three spy escapades. *Lili* had some nice music and comedy to recommend it, *Curtain* had a degree of suspense. All *The Tamarind Seed* really had was a glossy veneer and a hackneyed romance. The espionage background seemed more an excuse to keep the actors moving from exotic locale to exotic locale (Barbados, Paris, London, Canada) than to tell an absorbing story.

Usually writing his screenplays from scratch, Edwards based this on a novel by Evelyn Anthony. He was obviously not inspired by the material, as it seems a serviceable, if impersonal, treatment of a rather routine romantic novel. The film was a joint venture by three parties: Lew Grade's ITC Pictures (the only film to come from the television series/film agreement Julie had made in 1971), Lorimar Pictures, and Edwards. This was the first film of Julie's to have the whiff of British filmmaking all around it. For that reason, it was not accessible to American audiences as it might otherwise have been. (Her other British-made film was *Duet For One* in 1986.)

Julie's pairing with Sharif was effective, however, and for the first time she really advanced from an ingenue heroine to a mature woman in love. She looked beautiful in gowns designed by Dior befitting the film's jet-set ambience.

The film was a passable evening's entertainment, but gathered little public attention in its first release. Though it probably didn't harm Julie's career, it didn't provide a noticeable boost either. (She did not make another film after this until Edwards' *10* in 1979.)

Reviews

Variety (7/10/74) -- *Variety* felt there were two potential audiences for this film: those wanting a "love story with spy background or vice versa." The performances of Julie and Omar Sharif as "unlikely romantics" were seen as a "major strong point of the film." Also highly praised were the performances of Daniel O'Herlihy and Oscar Homolka, as well as the film's technical accomplishments.

New York Times (7/12/74) -- The main slant of the *Times* review was that Blake Edwards was so infatuated with his new wife that he was too busy making love to her with his camera to really think about making a film. The sarcastic tone of the review was typical of the way the press treated Edwards and Julie during this period. Unfortunately, the reviewer was too preoccupied with his determination to ridicule the couple to write a coherent critique. The film was said to be absorbed with "the chastity of its heroine." Julie was said to play a woman "who considers a goodnight kiss as the first, irrevocable step toward total degradation." At least, the reviewer found some faint praise for the supporting performers ("not at all bad."). Sharif's main function was said to be giving Julie her line cues. Julie was described as being "totally removed and above everything."

*****

F11   ***THE PINK PANTHER STRIKES AGAIN***
(United Artists; 1976; 103 minutes; Video: CBS/Fox))

Julie's sole contribution to this film is her voice, which is dubbed in for a male female impersonator in one sequence. See Appendix B for more details.

*****

F12   ***10***
(Orion Pictures; 1979; 122 minutes: Video: Warner)

Credits

Director/Screenplay	Blake Edwards
Producers	Blake Edwards
	Tony Adams
Music	Henry Mancini
Song lyrics	Carol Bayer Sager
	Robert Wells
Camera (Technicolor/Panavision)	Frank Stanley
Editor	Ralph E. Winters
Designer	Roger Maus
Set Decorators	Reg Allen
	Jack Stevens
Sound	Bruce Bisenz
Assistant Directors	Mickey McCardle
	Karen Murray
Costumes	Pat Edwards

Cast

George	Dudley Moore
Sam	Julie Andrews
Jenny	Bo Derek
Hugh	Robert Webber
Mary Lewis	Dee Wallace
David	Sam Jones
Bartender	Brian Dennehy
Reverend	Max Showalter

Josh	Rad Daily
Mrs. Kissel	Nedra Volt
Fred Miles	James Noble
Ethel Miles	Virginia Kiser
Covington	John Hawker
Dental Assistant	Deborah Rush
Neighbor	Don Calfa
Larry	Walter George Alton
Redhead	Annette Martin
Dr. Croce	John Hancock
TV Director	Larry Goldman
Pharmacist	Arthur Rosenberg
Waitress	Mari Gorman

Also March Hanson, Senilo Tanney, Kitty DeCarlo, Bill Lucking, Owen Sullivan, Debbie White, Laurence Carr, Camila Ashland, Burke Byrnes, Doug Sheehan, J. Victor Lopez, Jon Linton, John Chappel, Art Kassul

Synopsis

George is an Oscar-winning Los Angeles songwriter who, on the occasion of his forty-second birthday, is coming face-to-face with midlife crisis. He has a comfortable relationship with a successful singer, Samantha, a highly lucrative career, a beautiful home, and all of the trappings of the Southern California good life. But he has a restless spirit. He sees youth and vigor everywhere he looks except in his own back yard. He views the wild parties of his swinging neighbors through a telescope, receiving vicarious thrills watching the type of freewheeling lifestyle that he can only dream about.

Suddenly, the excitement he has been yearning for is promised one fateful day when he spots his perfect "11" (on a scale of 1-10). The gorgeous Jenny pulls up next to him at a stoplight, and he experiences pure unbridled passionate desire at first sight. He is overcome by an instant obsession to pursue this irresistible woman, at first not even realizing that it happens to be her wedding day. He follows her to the chapel and hides in the bushes, watching her take her wedding vows. She seems to embody all of the possibilities of adventurous youth that he wants at this point in his life, as compared to the steady maturity and predictable dependability of Samantha, which is admirable but unexciting to George.

Although Jenny is a brand new bride, George's obsession doesn't stop there. Discovering that her father is a dentist, he unnecessarily has several teeth filled just to get into the dentist's office to find out more about the woman who doesn't even know that he exists. After the painful ordeal, he learns that the newlyweds are honeymooning in Mexico.

After a fight with Samantha, who is losing patience with his immature and restless ways, George decides to follow the object of his pipe dream to Mexico to find out if a real romance is in his destiny.

Following a series of slapstick complications, George eventually finds himself in a romantic situation alone with Jenny in her hotel room, while Ravel's seductive *Bolero* plays on the phonograph. The scene is set for George to fulfill a fantasy that other men can only dream about.

However, before George gives in to his lustful temptations to make his fantasy a reality, he suddenly realizes it's better left as a fantasy. As much as he's like to, he simply can't go through with it.

He leaves his perfect "11" behind, returns to the less exciting but dependable Samantha and decides to make a stab at creating excitement at home -- to the tune of Ravel's *Bolero*.

Commentary

Julie's first film after a five-year sabbatical was something quite different for her -- a sexy role in an adult comedy. Although it was actually a supporting role, with Julie playing second fiddle to Dudley Moore, it still provided a sorely needed career boost.

Julie managed to shed her goody-goody image naturally for the first time -- no self-conscious bare breast scenes were needed. She simply played a mature, well rounded role as called for and proved she could deliver the goods.

The film was also Edwards' first genuine hit aside from the *Pink Panther* films in a long time. It was to signal a return to more serious, introspective films for him (*S.O.B., The Man Who Loved Women, That's Life!*), alternating over the next several years with his traditional slapstick comedies (*Micky and Maude, A Fine Mess, Blind Date*). The theme of midlife crisis was a thread running through most of his films from this period -- farces and serious comedies alike.

The biggest flaw of *10* is one that has dogged Edwards for years -- everything from *Darling Lili* to *That's Life!* He cannot seem to sustain a sensitive comedy-drama without throwing in totally inappropriate slapstick humor. This is especially evident in *10*, which at its best is a literate, touching, intelligent, and substantial comedy of considerable resonance. Many of Moore's antics are sidesplitting -- no doubt about that. But they belong in another film. Even in his best work (*Victor/Victoria, That's Life!*), Edwards is a self-indulgent, ham-handed director at times, who would benefit greatly by taking advice from an outside observer who could see the excesses and help him judiciously edit his own work.

Nonetheless, *10* was full of good things. Sensitively played by both Moore and Julie, the midlife crisis theme has seldom been played out more poignantly. In typical Edwards fashion, the supporting cast -- Robert Webber, Brian Dennehy, Dee Wallace, Max Showalter, yes, even Bo Derek are first-rate. And -- appropriate or not -- one has to admit that Edwards still rolls out sight gags along with the best of them.

The lead role was originally earmarked for George Segal, who allegedly quit because Julie's role was expanded. With due respect to George Segal, he did not do moviegoers a disservice. Neither did he harm Dudley Moore, because this is the role that made Moore an American film star. It was a pleasure to have Julie back in a quality film, even though she wasn't the star. Next to *Victor/Victoria*, this is the finest film she has done for Blake Edwards.

Julie sang Henry Mancini's songs "He Pleases Me" and "It's Easy to Say" (an Oscar nominee), first as a duet with Moore, then as a solo.

Reviews

Variety (9/26/79) -- The *Variety* reacion to this film was pure *boffo*. Blake Edwards' "best pic in years" was described as "a shrewdly observed and beautifully executed comedy of manners and morals." Both Dudley Moore and Edwards were said to be in "top slapstick form." The "dialog-heavy scenes" between Julie and Moore were called "well structured." However, Julie was called "rather miscast" in what was termed "a very cold, serious part." Moore was accorded the bulk of the reviewer's credit for the film's success.

New York Times (10/5/79) -- The *Times* found this comedy "frequently hilarious." Like *Variety*, the *Times* felt like Moore was the clear standout in the film. He was said to be funny "without ever having to appear stupid." The reviewer compared Edwards' salute to Moore to the director's valentine to Julie in *Darling Lili*, both clearly vehicles that were expressly tailored for a particular star. Julie's "no-nonsense presence" was said to be an important part of the comedy, despite the brevity of her role. She was called "the light at the end of the tunnel of George's midlife crisis." The film was described as being "loaded with odd surprises."

*****

F13   *LITTLE MISS MARKER*
         (Universal; 1980; 103 minutes; Video: MCA)

Credits
Based on a story by Damon Runyon
Director/Screenplay	Walter Bernstein
Producer	Jennings Lang
Camera (Technicolor)	Philip Lathrop
Designer	Edward C. Carfagno
Set Decoration	Hal Gausman
Editor	Eve Newman
Music	Henry Mancini
Assistant Directors	Ronald J. Martinez
	Judith Vogelsang

Cast
Sorrowful Jones	Walter Matthau
Amanda	Julie Andrews
Blackie	Tony Curtis
Regret	Bob Newhart
The Judge	Lee Grant
"The Kid"	Sara Stimson
Herbie	Brian Dennehy
Brannigan	Kenneth McMillan
Carter	Andrew Rubin
Benny	Joshua Shelly
Clerk	Randy Herman
Mrs. Clancy	Nedra Volz
Lola	Jacquelyn Hyde
Vittorio	Tom Pedi
Clerk	Jessica Rains
Teller	Henry Slate
Morris	Alvin Hammer
Sam	Don Bexley
Manager	Jack DeLeon
Clerk	John P. Finnegan

Also Ralph Manza, Jack Mullaney, Mark Anger, Lennie Bremen, Maurice Marks, Colin Gilbert, Wynn Irwin, Joseph Knowland, Stanley Lawrence, Louis Basile, Ed Ness, H.B. Newton, Stanley E. Ritchie, William Ackridge, Alan Thomason, Charles A. Venegas, Sharri Zak, Robert E. Ball, Simmy Bow, Jorge B. Cruz

Synopsis
        In Depression-era New York, Sorrowful Jones is a gruff, unmarried gambler trying to keep one step ahead of the mobsters who he regularly does business with. He very abruptly becomes guardian to an adorable 6-year old girl. The girl (known only as "The Kid") is initially left with Jones to hold for security while her father scrapes together the money owed to Jones for a gambling debt.
        When Jones discovers that her father has been killed, he must hang on to his little "asset" until he decides what to do with her. Before he realizes what's happening, the Kid is winning him over, gradually turning the curmudgeonly hustler into a docile teddy bear.

Amanda is the socialite widow who develops a friendship and affection for both Sorrowful and the Kid, but she begins to question his suitability as a parent. His criminal business associates and less-than-homey lifestyle do not strike Amanda as a suitable environment for raising a young girl.

The story climaxes in a courtroom custody battle for the Kid between Amanda and Sorrowful. The result of the unusual courtroom discussions is a family union for the threesome, providing a wife and daughter for Sorrowful, and a happy homelife for the Kid.

Commentary

After a return to form in *10*, Julie's film career hit the skids again in her very next film. The "inspiration" for this film was a creaky 1934 Shirley Temple/Damon Runyon vehicle that had already been recycled through two remakes (Bob Hope and Lucille Ball in *Sorrowful Jones*, and Tony Curtis and Suzanne Pleshette in *Forty Pounds of Trouble*). There was scarcely a pressing cinematic need for a fourth treatment.

Though the film was not an embarrassment -- it was mildly amusing and beautifully mounted -- it was not a strong career boost for Julie. Even more so than in *10*, this was a supporting role -- not a starring one -- for her. Though she played the romantic lead opposite top-billed Walter Matthau, she clearly played second fiddle to Matthau and cute moppet Sara Stimson in the title role. This is a *gruff man-warms-up-to-little-girl* story -- not an adult romantic comedy.

Julie seemed to appear onscreen for little more than a half an hour, and her presence was incidental to the main action most of the way through. The part -- a rich heiress who raised horses -- was blandly written and had no dimension. It didn't even have the saccharine quality of her early film roles. Even that may have been more interesting than the character presented here.

Although the production values are top-notch and the cast is strong (Matthau, Tony Curtis, Bob Newhart, Lee Grant), it's a little puzzling why Julie got involved in the project. Her judgement of roles suited to her and scripts that would work for her was usually better. Universal, probably well aware that audiences would be apathetic, released the film more as a low-budget programmer than the grade A production that it was. Predictably, it had a very short theatrical run, and is probably not recalled by anyone except devout Matthau or Andrews fans.

Little Sara Stimson in the Shirley Temple role was an unqualifed delight. (One wonders what ever happened to her.) As the film begins, a jaunty Henry Mancini score promises a sense of fun reminiscent of *The Sting*, but screenwriter Walter Bernstein (in his directing debut) never delivers on that promise. Matthau, more subdued than usual, was not at his best in a sterotypical role for him. Even pros Curtis and Newhart were flat in the promising roles of a mobster and Matthau's sidekick, respectively. Lee Grant was wasted in a bit part as a judge.

Hopefully Hollywood will now let this tired 30s relic rest in peace.

Reviews

Variety (3/19/80) -- "What price, Damon Runyon?" was *Variety's* headline for this review, implying disservice to the Runyon short story on which the film was based. Walter Bernstein was said to "blow his directorial debut completely." The reviewer felt that Walter Matthau was a great choice to play the Sorrowful Jones character, causing the film's failure to be regrettable. The casting of Julie ("with her British accent") was criticized, as the reviewer felt the flavor of 1934 Broadway was lost in the process. Young moppett Sara Stimson, in her film debut as the title character, was said to be "the only really decent thing about the picture." The relationship between Matthau and the little girl is said to remain undeveloped and "contrived." The romance between Matthau and Julie is also termed a failure. Feeling that Julie's character was "beyond the original story," the reviewer found her attraction to

Matthau less than credible. The visual elements of the film, if nothing else, impressed the reviewer as "first-rate."

New York Times (3/21/80) --The *Times* found disparity between Runyon's "sentimental tale" and the movie's tone, which was "relatively cool." Unlike *Variety*, the *Times* didn't find much to get enthusiastic about in young Sara Stimson's performance. Walter Matthau was found to be "better at being gruff than at being fond." The reviewer was amused by some of the dialogue adapted by Walter Bernstein from Damon Runyon's material, and enjoyed some of the running gags. But the overall film was termed "expensively listless much of the time." Julie was said to "look lovely" in costumes designed by Ruth Morley with her "natural hauteur...somehow softened by the role."

*****

F14   *S.O.B.*
          (Paramount; 1981; 121 minutes; Video: CBS/Fox)

Credits

Director/Screenplay	Blake Edwards
Producers	Blake Edwards
	Tony Adams
Camera (Metrocolor/Panavision)	Harry Stradling
Designer	Roger Maus
Editor	Ralph E. Winters
Music	Henry Mancini
Executive Producer	Michael B. Wolf
Associate Producer	Gerald T. Nutting
Art Director	William Craig Smith
Costumes	Theodora Van Runkle
Choreographer	Paddy Stone
Assistant Directors	L. Andrew Stone
	Emmitt-Leon O'Neill

Cast

Sally Miles	Julie Andrews
Tim Culley	William Holden
Mavis	Marisa Berenson
Dick Benson	Larry Hagman
Herb Maskowitz	Robert Loggia
Gary Murdock	Stuart Margolin
Felix Farmer	Richard Mulligan
Dr. Irving Finegarten	Robert Preston
Willard	Craig Stevens
Polly Reid	Loretta Swit
David Blackman	Robert Vaughan
Ben Coogan	Robert Webber
Eva Brown	Shelley Winters
Lila	Jennifer Edwards
Capitol Studios Vice-President	John Pleshette
Guard	Ken Swofford
Chinese Chef	Benson Fong
Guru	Larry Storch
Mortician	Byron Kane

Jogger	Stiffe Tanney
Babs	Rosanna Arquette
Capitol Studios Vice-President	John Lawlor
Lab Manager	Hamilton Camp
Gardener	Burt Rosario
Sam Marshall	David Young
Mortician's Wife	Virginia Gregg
Tammy Taylor	Kathleen MacMurray
Barker	Paddy Stone
Clive Lytell	Gene Nelson

Also Joe Penny, Stephen Johnson, Pat Colbert, Erica Yohn, Charles Lampkin, Kevin Justrich, Kimberly Woodward, Scott Arthur Allen, Corbin Bernsen, Joseph Benti, Rebecca Edwards, Neil Flanagan, Todd Howland, Jill Jaress, Alexandra Johnson, Len Lawson, Shelby Leverington, Gisele Lindley, Dominick Mazzie, Fay McKenzie, Bill McLaughlin, Tony Miller, Dave Morick, Charles Park, Charles Roewe, James Purcell, Gay Rowan, Borah Silver, Ken Smolka, Henry Sutton, Noel Toy, Howard Vann, Sharri Zak

Synopsis

A famous Hollywood director, Felix Farmer, has just released a multimillion dollar bomb of a film musical called *Night Wind*. To add insult to injury, the film stars his Academy Award winning (for *Peter Pan*) wife, Sally Miles, America's G-rated family musical sweetheart.

A group of manipulative, greedy moguls at the studio that produced the fiasco are trying to think of ways to re-edit the film in an attempt to salvage it. Sally decides to leave Felix in the midst of all this chaos, and ultimately Felix suffers a nervous breakdown. He also bungles several ill-fated attempts to commit suicide.

Felix finally hits upon the brainstorm of reshooting the film as a pornographic musical. To ensure success, he feels he must persuade Sally to bring in the boxoffice throngs by discarding her goody-two shoes image and baring her breasts for the camera. Helped along by the intervention of a greedy agent and other sleazy characters, Sally is persuaded to do the film, nude scene and all.

All seems to be going well until Felix and the studio disagree over the editing of the final release version. Felix attempts to steal the negatives of the picture, but is shot down and killed by a police officer.

A group of Farmer's buddies steal his body from the mortuary, and ultimately set it aflame at sea in a Viking-style funeral.

Commentary

As *S.O.B.* begins, Julie Andrews fans are likely to think they've entered H. G. Wells' *Time Machine* and ended up back in the mid-60s. What *is* this? Sixteen years after *The Sound of Music*, Julie Andrews singing "Polly Wolly Doodle" in a G-rated family musical? But wait...Julie was never this sappy, her fantasy films were never this juvenile. By the time the credits have finished rolling, anyone who wasn't in on the joke when they bought their ticket has figured it out: this is a *satire* of Hollywood moviemaking -- not the real thing. And Julie, bless her G-rated heart, is poking fun at her own public image. And boy would she *really* poke fun, halfway through the film when she pulls off her blouse to reveal bare "boobies."

This scene, in fact, was the most ill-advised of Edwards' attempts to present his wife as a sex goddess. Even though on the surface, he and Julie appeared to be good-naturedly kidding her screen image, the gambit seemed self-conscious, beneath her dignity, and totally unnecessary. Neither comic nor dramatically relevant, it was simply exploitative and embarrassing. While she's a versatile actress and an attractive performer, this type of sexpot career slant is as unsuitable for Julie as was Miss Goody-Goody. Thankfully, she has never done anything this distasteful on the screen ever since.

Eleven years after *Darling Lili* was released, *S.O.B.* was Blake Edwards attempt to get back at the Hollywood brass, who he fought with tooth and nail, regarding his and Julie's film *Darling Lili* and the William Holden western *Wild Rovers*. And Edwards came back with a vengeance. *S.O.B.* was one of the most bitter, cynical, mean-spirited comedies ever to be released by a Hollywood studio (ironically by Paramount, who produced *Darling Lili*).

That alone would have made *S.O.B.* a questionable boxoffice prospect. But the final boxoffice knell was probably dealt by the film's unending esoterica. Unless you had a far greater than average knowledge of personalities, events, and inside jokes in Hollywood, most of the film probably sailed right over your proverbial head. Satire may not *always* close in Peoria, but satire this regional probably does.

Nevertheless, the film has its admirers. Like other Edwards projects, a cult of devotees (including some of the major media reviewers) cheered the film on when it was initially released, and continue to promote it as a classic of sorts. It's not a film that's likely to age well. If the satire wasn't understood by many moviegoers in the early 1980s, it's not likely to become more relevant into the 90s or beyond.

Reviews
Variety (6/24/81) -- *Variety* called this manic farce "occasionally hilarious...a wildly mixed bag of blessings," suggesting that the film's satiric pitch towards "Hollywood's insider sensibilities" was likely to escape the average audience's understanding. Only a few characters were said to "maintain a solid base," including Julie's "pragmatic prima donna," Robert Preston's "Dr. Feelgood type," the "sanely lecherous director" played by William Holden, and the "ulcerous press agent" of Robert Webber. The major problem was stated to be the overacting of Richard Mulligan as the despondent director, with his "eye-rolling, manic-depressive mugging."

New York Times (6/28/81) -- The *Times* apparently found this film somewhat of a paradox, condemning it and praising it to the skies almost in the same breath. It was said to be "a nasty, biased, self-serving movie," yet it was also described as "hilarious most of the time." It was "mean-spirited" yet "consistently funny." Julie was called "utterly charming." The performances were called "wickedly right." Singled out as "especially fine" were Julie, William Holden, Robert Preston, Stuart Margolin, and Loretta Swit. Blake Edwards' direction was called "as furious as his screenplay is funny."

*****

F15   *VICTOR/VICTORIA*
(MGM; 1982; 133 minutes; Video: MGM/UA)

Credits
Based on the 1933 German film *Victor Und Viktoria* by Rheinhold Schuenzel and Hans Hoemburg

Director/Screenplay	Blake Edwards
Producers	Blake Edwards
	Tony Adams
Music	Henry Mancini
Lyrics	Leslie Bricusse
Camera (Panavision/Metrocolor)	Dick Bush
Editor	Ralph E. Winters
Designer	Roger Maus
Art Directors	Tim Hutchinson

	William Craig Smith
Set Design	Harry Cordwell
Costumes	Patricia Norris
Choreographer	Paddy Stone
Assistant Directors	Richard Hoult
	Peter Kohn
	Paul Tivers
Associate Producer	Gerald T. Nutting

Cast

Victor/Victoria	Julie Andrews
King	James Garner
Toddy	Robert Preston
Norma	Lesley Ann Warren
Squash	Alex Karras
Cassel	John Rhys-Davies
Waiter	Graham Stark
Labisse	Peter Arne
Bovin	Sherloque Tanney
Hotel Manager	Michael Robbins
Sal	Norman Chancer
Restaurant Manager	David Gant
Madame President	Maria Charles
Richard	Malcolm Jamieson
Juke	John Cassady
Clam	Mike Terzcan
Stage Manager	Christopher Good
Cassell's Receptionist	Matyelock Gibbs
Guy Langois	Jay Benedict
Langois' Companion	Oliver Pierre
Concierge	Martin Rayner
Fat Man with Eclair	George Silver
Large Lady in restaurant	Joanna Dickens
Deviant Husband	Terence Skelton
Simone Kallisto	Ina Skriver
Boyfriend to actress	Stuart Turton
Police Inspector	Geoffrey Beevers
Chorus Boys	Sam Williams
	Simon Chandler
Nightclub M.C.	Neil Cunningham
Chambermaid	Vivienne Chandler
LeClou	Bill Monks
Balancing Man	Perry Davey
Opera Singer	Elizabeth Vaughan
Photographer	Paddy Ward
Desk Clerk	Tim Stern

Synopsis

Toddy is an aging gay nightclub singer in 1934 Paris. One evening when Toddy is performing, his estranged male lover, Richard (an opportunistic hustler), enters the club, and Toddy tosses a few sarcastic barbs at his lover's party of friends. A brawl ensues and the club owner subsequently fires Toddy.

Also down on her luck is Victoria Grant, a trained soprano whose voice is too pristine for the demands of the local night spots. Evicted from her hotel room due to nonpayment of rent, a hungry and desperate Victoria enters a local restaurant and orders two full-course meals. Her plan is to plant a cockroach in her plate as she finishes eating the second meal, thus avoiding paying the check.

Toddy enters the restaurant. Recognizing Victoria from one of her unsuccessful auditions, he speaks to her. She invites him to join her for dinner, letting him in on her plot to secure a free meal. She tries the ruse, but it appears that the restaurant manager is not going to let the duo get away with their scheme. Suddenly, the cockroach crawls up a fat woman's leg, and a wild melee ensues. Toddy and Victoria take advantage of the confusion to slip outside and rush to Toddy's apartment in a downpouring rain.

After admitting that he is gay, Toddy invites Victoria to spend a platonic night at his apartment, realizing she has nowhere else to go. When Victoria tries to get into her dress the next morning, she discovers to her dismay that it has shrunk from the drenching. She puts on Toddy's suit, which suddenly gives Toddy a wild idea.

To provide needed employment for himself and Victoria, he launches a scheme to pass Victoria off to local club owners as a gay male who performs as a female impersonator. He gambles that the scheme is just bizarre enough to work, and he is right. After being rigorously coached by Toddy, Victoria rapidly gains employment at a local nightclub..

One evening while Victoria is performing, a Chicago mobster called King comes in to see the show, accompanied by his featherbrained moll Norma and his bodyguard, Squash. King is instantly attracted to Victoria, not realizing she is (supposedly) a male. He is quite taken aback when she pulls off her wig at the end of the act.

After the performance, Victoria meets King. Somewhat turned off by his homophobic arrogance, she hits the nail on the head when she implies that he is confused about his own emotions. He could never find another man attractive, now could he?

Tired of Norma's empty-headed, shrill haranguing, King sends her back to Chicago. Soon thereafter, King learns that Victoria is really a woman. The two of them fall in love. Meanwhile, Squash (who will eventually admit that he is gay), watches in amazement as his macho touch guy boss appears to be having an affair with another man.

Victoria does not want her masquerade exposed, because it will endanger her job, so she and King diligently strive to keep their romance a secret. In the ensuing labyrinth of comic complications, everyone's notions of male/female relationships are turned topsy turvy. The confusion reaches its peak when Norma returns from Chicago and launches a scheme to get even with King.

About the time that Victoria and King decide that their romance is doomed to failure due to the odds stacked against it, Victoria decides to end the charade and reveals her true gender. Romance for Victoria and King wins out.

Toddy dons wig, dress, and heels in the comic finale, taking to the stage as the new "Victoria," finally providing a *genuine* imposter for the club, as opposed to the make-believe imposter.

For a list of musical numbers, see the Discography section (**D37**).

Commentary

This is the best of all of the film collaborations between Julie and her producer/director husband Blake Edwards. This was largely because Edwards finally returned Julie to her forte -- the musical comedy. *Victor/Victoria* proved that a good film musical could still deliver at the boxoffice -- even in the austere movie marketplace of the cynical 80s.

Though it suffers from a few chronic Edwardsisms -- excessive length, belabored slapstick, confusion among conflicting genres -- the film was a genuine triumph for Julie, earning her a second Best Actress Oscar nomination. (She lost to Meryl Streep in *Sophie's Choice*.) And the vehicle itself was substantial enough to withstand the directorial excesses.

While the basic plot premise was somewhat risque (a-down-on-her-luck female singer masquerades as a gay female impersonator), the form of the film was traditional farce. Like *La Cage Aux Folles*, the film presented a controversial theme as a mere backdrop for what is essentially a wholesome comedy.

In fact, one wishes Edwards had pursued the interesting sexual identity theme with a bit more depth. The few moments that delve into character reflection of the questions raised by the sexual masquerade gambit are so intelligently written and played that it's a shame there aren't more thought-provoking moments.

Nevertheless, the theme is treated more profoundly here than it was in *Tootsie* (and a bit less so than in *Yentl*). It adds a touch of substance to the generally featherweight froth.

Though its a delight to see Julie in a musical comedy format again, the songs by Henry Mancini (music)/Leslie Bricusse (lyrics) unfortunately lack pizzazz, and do not really add to the sophisticated, zany mood. The middle-of-the -road banality of Henry Mancini's work served Blake Edwards much better in the seriocomic *Breakfast at Tiffany's* and the melodramatic *Days of Wine and Roses*.

With *Victor/Victoria*, the material is so ripe for a bouncy, ribald musical score along the lines of Broadway's French import *Irma La Douce* that one wishes a veteran Broadway tunesmith like Jerry Herman (*La Cage Aux Folles, Hello Dolly!, Mame*) had been enlisted for the project. Nonetheless, Julie has one lovely ballad, "Crazy World," and a charming soft shoe duet number with Robert Preston, "You and Me."

Despite the missed musical opportunities, Edwards' Parisian fable plays like vintage Billy Wilder comedy-- spicy, slightly naughty, worldly and wise. The screenplay is based on a German comedy from the 30s called *Victor und Viktoria*, skillfully adapted in this new script by Edwards.

Adding to the effectiveness of the project is a spectacular cast. In one of his last screen roles, Robert Preston complements Julie beautifully in the role of her warm and wonderful gay pal Toddy. Julie is also reteamed with James Garner for the first time since *The Americanization of Emily* (1964). In the romantic leading role of the macho, but confused, mobster from Chicago, Garner is in top form. Lesley Ann Warren almost steals the show as Garner's pinheaded moll from Chicago, copping a Supporting Actress nomination in the process.

Julie, of course, is right at home with the project and seems to be having as much fun as the audience One could criticize the fact that she doesn't bring more of a sardonic twist to the musical numbers. As Gene Siskel pointed out when he reviewed the show on the PBS *Sneak Previews* show (March 1982), she's basically just Julie Andrews singing. There appears to be no attempt to suggest the double irony of a woman pretending to be a man pretending to be a woman. Nonetheless, her comic timing was at its best since *Thoroughly Modern Millie*, and the role was effective enough to put her on the Oscar roster.

Though Julie's dramatic acting asserted itself more powerfully than ever in two 1986 films (*That's Life!* and *Duet For One*), she hasn't had an unqualified film triumph or a boxoffice hit since *Victor/Victoria*.

Reviews

Variety (3/17/82) -- The major trade paper enthusiastically called the film "a sparkling, ultra-sophisticated entertainment...a beautifully produced effort." Praise was found for the "sharp performances and nice musical numbers." Robert Preston was termed "most impressive of all." The role of Victoria was seen to be Julie's "most rewarding" in years. The paper was pleased to see her in a musical comedy format "more sophisticated than the pictures that made her name in the 1960s." The paper's only real reservation was overlength.

New York Times (3/19/82) -- The *Times* was as positive as *Variety* in evaluating the film ("an unqualified hit"). Julie was seen to be "at the peak of her comic and singing form." The reviewer even compared her to Marlene Dietrich. Robert Preston was called " flawlessly funny." There was also ample praise for James Garner, Lesley Ann Warren, and Alex Karras.

*****

F16   ***THE MAN WHO LOVED WOMEN***
      (Columbia; 1983; 110 minutes; RCA/Columbia)

<u>Credits</u>
Based on Francois Truffaut's 1977 French film

Director	Blake Edwards
Producers	Blake Edwards
	Tony Adams
Screenplay	Blake Edwards
	Milton Wexler
	Geoffrey Edwards
Camera (Metrocolor)	Haskell Wexler
Designer	Roger Maus
Editor	Ralph E. Winters
Executive Producer	Jonathan D. Krane
Associate Producer	Gerald T. Nutting
Costumes	Ann Roth
Music	Henry Mancini
Song by	Henry Mancini
	Alan Bergman
	Marilyn Bergman
Sung by	Helen Reddy
Assistant Directors	Mickey McCardle
	Joseph Paul Moore
	Kevin A. Finnegan
Art Director	Jack Senter
Set Designers	Dianne I. Wagner
	Jacques Valin

<u>Cast</u>

David	Burt Reynolds
Marianna	Julie Andrews
Louise	Kim Basinger
Agnes	Marilu Henner
Courtney	Cynthia Sikes
Nancy	Jennifer Edwards
Janet	Sela Ward
Svetlana	Ellen Bauer
Enid	Denise Crosby
Legs	Tracy Vacarro
Roy	Barry Corbin
Al	Ben Powers
Sue	Jill Carroll
Doctor	Schweitzer Tanney
Regis Philbin	Himself
Dr. Simon Abrams	Joseph Bernard
Henry	John F. Flynn, Jr.
Carl	Jim Knaub
Lt. Cranzano	Jim Lewis
Sgt. Stone	Roger Rose

David's Mother — Jennifer Ashley
David at 16 — Tony Brown
David at 12 — Philip Alexander
David at 8 — Jonathan Rogal
Aerobics Instructor — Margie Denecke
Man at barbeque — Jerry Martin
Nurses — Sharon Hughes
Nanci Rogers
Darla — Cindo Dietrich

Also Kai J. Wong, Walter Soo Hoo, Marilyn Child, Arnie Moore, Lisa Blake Richards, Noni White, Lynn Webb, Jason Ross, Alisa Lee, Los Angeles Ballet

Synopsis

At the funeral of famous sculptor David Fowler, his psychiatrist and lover, Marianna, reminisces on the troubled life of a woebegotten playboy. In flashback, we discover that David was a middle-aged-man in search of happiness. In fact, he was so fervently in search of that ever-elusive prize that he was the male counterpart of a nymphomaniac. He loved all women, but he loved them one at a time.

Marianna recalls the day David first came to her for psychoanalysis. His stories of various romantic adventures were varied and sometimes quite remarkable.

Chief among the women in his past was Louise, the bored and kinky wife of a Houston millionaire. She loved to court danger and public exposure during her lovemaking. This eventually led to a series of comic complications the day her husband came home unexpectedly and David had to hide in her closet.

In the process of shrinking David's head, Marianna soon realizes that she is also falling for his charms. David has met an understanding and sophisticated new woman who perhaps will be the one to capture him and end his womanizing ways. But alas, David suddenly meets with an untimely demise.

The film ends as it began, with David's parade of past lovers mourning the passing of a man who loved too much...or perhaps never really loved at all.

Commentary

Neither Julie nor Blake Edwards can count *The Man Who Loved Women* among their best achievements. And that goes even more so for Burt Reynolds, the supposed star of this lethargic muddle of a film. This plodding, incoherent mess could be a perfect cure for insomnia.

Some scenes in this film, particularly the long, laborious psychoanalytic session at the beginning, are so slow-paced that one sometimes has the feeling the actors were taking naps between the lines. After introducing this deadly tone, Edwards eventually mixes in his customary slapstick, leaving the audience totally baffled as to whether this is supposed to be a Ingmar Bergman-style dirge or a Jerry Lewis yuckfest.

It's difficult to comment much on Julie's performance in this, because there's so little energy or coherency in the film that the actors might as well be reciting the telephone book. She looks attractive and seems to be approaching the proceedings in her usual professional manner, but she, like everyone else in the film, seems to be delivering her lines through a long, hollow tunnel.

The film may have damaged Julie's career if enough people had seen it to make any difference. Julie's sense of professionalism is usually so strong that it's impossible to imagine her not knowing this was a turkey during the filming. The film may not say anything one way or the other about her acting capability, but the fact that she stuck with it says an awful lot about her family loyalty.

Reviews

Variety (12/14/83) -- *Variety* had little positive to say about this film, which the paper termed "truly woeful, reeking of production-line, big star filmmaking and nothing else." Complaining of a slow start in the long, rambling scene with Julie psychoanalyzing the Burt Reynolds character, the reviewer felt that the film would never get started. Subsequently, he felt the film generated "the equally unpleasant feeling that it [would] never end."

New York Times (12/16/83) -- The *Times* had a considerably more favorable reaction to this film than *Variety* (or just about any other paper). Also complaining about a slow start, the paper felt that once the film got going, it "[skated] successfully over thin ice." Reynolds' performance was called the film's greatest virtue ("the most consistently funny, disciplined performance that...[he] has yet done"). The reviewer, however, did not feel that the film represented Blake Edwards at his best. Praising Reynolds' female costars, who were said to "give Mr. Reynolds a run for his money," both Kim Basinger (as the promiscuous wife of a millionaire) and Julie as his psychiatrist/ lover found favor with the *Times*. According to the reviewer, Julie was good at listening (which was a lot of what this role called for), but "far more entertaining as an all-out comedienne."

*****

F17   *THAT'S LIFE*!
         (Columbia; 1986; 102 minutes; Video: Vestron)

Credits

Director	Blake Edwards
Producer	Tony Adams
Screenplay	Milton Wexler
	Blake Edwards
Music	Henry Mancini
Song by	Henry Mancini (music)
	Leslie Bricusse (lyrics)
Sung by	Tony Bennet
Camera (DeLuxe Color/Panavision)	Anthony Richmond
Editor	Lee Rhoads
Executive Producer	Joseph D. Krane
Associate Producers	Trish Caroselli
	Connie McCauley
Production Manager	Alan Levine
Assistant Directors	Alan Levine
	K.C. Colwell
Costumes	Traci Tynan
Music Supervision	Al Bunetta
	Tom Bocci
Production Coordinator	Carrie Dieterich
Sound	Don Sumner
Set Decoration	Tony Marando

Cast

Harvey Fairchild	Jack Lemmon
Gillian Fairchild	Julie Andrews
Holly Parrish	Sally Kellerman

Father Baragone	Robert Loggia
Megan Fairchild Bartlet	Jennifer Edwards
Steve Larwin	Rob Knepper
Larry Bartlet	Matt Lattanzi
Josh Fairchild	Chris Lemmon
Janice Kern	Cynthia Sikes
Fanny Ward	Dana Sparks
Kate Fairchild	Emma Walton
Madame Carrie	Felicia Farr
Corey	Theodore Wilson
Andre	Nicky Blair
Dr. Keith Romanis	Jordan Christopher
Belmont	Biff Elliot
Phil Carlson	Hal Riddle
Harold	Harold Harris
Jesse Grant	Jess G. Henecke
Lisa	Lisa Kingston
Dr. Gerald Spelner	Dr. Charles Scheiner
Chutney	Chutney Walton
Honey	Honey Edwards

Also Sherry P. Sievert, Joe Lopez, James Umphlett, Frann Bradford, Ken Gehrig, Donna McMullen, Scott L. McKenna, Cora Bryant, Robin Foster, Eddie Vail, Deborah Figuly, Larry Holt, Gene Hartline, Ernie Anderson, Harry Birrell

Synopsis

When Gillian Fairchild must have a biopsy to analyze a growth of tissue in her throat, she keeps the news from her family. Unfortunately, she will have to bear the solitary worry for an entire weekend, because the lab results won't be in until the following week. This would be a difficult enough set of circumstances as it is, but Gillian's plight is even worse because she is a professional singer.

While keeping her own perfectly understandable worries to herself, Gillian ironically has to put up with the whining and neurotic paranoia of her hypochondriac husband, Harvey. Harvey is suffering an acute case of fear of aging and inflicts his incessant fatalistic philosophies on everyone around him.

One by one, the three Fairchild children arrive for the father's 60th birthday celebration, which is to take place at the family's Malibu home that weekend. Daughter Kate is pining over the breakup with her boyfriend Steve. Shortly after Kate arrives, their pregnant daughter Megan shows up with her husband Larry Bartlet, followed by their son Josh, a television actor, and his girl friend Fanny.

Harvey alienates the family with his unpleasant, moody attitude at a family dinner. Meanwhile, he has ignored the suggestion by his physician that he is physically healthy but should see a psychiatrist. Instead, Harvey visits a psychic, Madame Carrie, who seduces him. It isn't until he is encouraged by his confessor priest Father Baragone to take the pulpit with a sermon on adultery that he suddenly realizes he has contacted a case of crabs. He twitches and itches before a chapel full of parishioners, while pontificating on the evils of marital infidelity.

Meanwhile, Gillian prepares for the birthday party while she tries to console heartbroken Kate, whose trauma is suddenly over when boyfriend Steve shows up. Gillian also has to soothe Megan, who has fears about her pregnancy. All the while that Gillian is mothering everyone (including Harvey), she is bearing the burden of her biopsy all by herself.

In the midst of the party, she finally has had it with Harvey's irrational complaining and she tells him he's either going to have to get ahold of himself and stop the insane bellyaching or she will leave him. That seems to do the trick, and Harvey seems to realize how foolish he's been. At that moment, Gillian receives news that the growth was benign. She is finally able to share the news, but is triumphant that it is happy news indeed.

Commentary

That's Life! featured Julie's most effective dramatic performance up to its time (until *Duet For One*, which arrived three months later). The fact that it's a subtle, carefully shaded role rather than a showy star turn is even more impressive.

In this film, Edwards explores the midlife crisis theme that he presented so successfully in *10*, and finds new degrees of insight and intelligence. Despite his customary lapses into inappropriate slapstick and heavy-handed humor, this is one of Edwards' darkest, most introspective films.

In seeking out truly unbiased film criticism, one question that I have often pondered is whether too much background information on a film spoils it's chances of critical success. (One could probably write a whole book on that topic regarding *Darling Lili*, but that's another story.) One very common critical complaint aimed at *That's Life!* was the fact that it was a family affair. (It was filmed in the Andrews/Edwards Malibu home. In the cast are their children Jennifer Edwards and Emma Walton. Jack Lemmon's wife, Felicia Farr, and son, Chris Lemmon are also in the cast. Much of the script was reportedly improvised during filming.) So what? Why can't a film be judged by what's up on the screen? When John Cassavettes does the very same thing, he gets critical raves.

If this is what it took to get such a moving, deeply personal film out of Edwards, so be it. The film has some shattering moments and leaves a lingering feeling of deep melancholy that few modern Hollywood films can match.

It also provides Julie one of her most spectacular scenes to date -- a climatic encounter that solidifies the film in a unique and profound way. Julie was touted for an Oscar nomination for this, and should have received it. With minimal dialogue and a subtle role, she manges to anchor the whole film and provide it with a depth of feeling that a lesser actress may have missed. She obviously responds well to Edwards' direction.

Reviews

Variety (9/3/86) -- This early review by the film industry's major trade paper was one of the very best that the film received. Comparing the film to *10*, which had been about midlife crisis, the reviewer saw *That's Life!* as Blake Edwards' "freak-out over the prospect of entering old age." Noting the highly personal nature of the film, the reviewer felt that the film was "thoroughly absorbing and entertaining except for a few dud scenes" (a common complaint about Edwards' films). Jack Lemmon's lead performance was termed "terrific." However, the out-of-place slapstick bothered the reviewer. To him, the gags often came across as "gratuitous and desperately thrown in." Julie was said to complement Lemmon's acting beautifully. In final analysis, the reviewer found the film to "stick to the ribs" because of its deep feelings and "unlike most Hollywood product these days, is actually *about* something."

New York Times (9/26/86) -- The *Times* cautioned viewers that the film was so positive and sunny on the surface that "its worried psyche is obscured much of the time." Nonetheless, it was seen as possibly Blake Edwards' "most somber comedy to date." While Lemmon's role was seen as the "flashiest," Julie was said to dominate the film. Unlike the nasty and sarcastic slams the *Times* made against Julie and Edwards as a husband/wife filmmaking team when *The Tamarind Seed* was reviewed, the paper now viewed Edwards' obvious affection for his wife as a positive influence on the film.

*****

F18   *DUET FOR ONE*
            (Cannon; 1986; 107 minutes; Video: MGM/UA)

<u>Credits</u>
Based on the play by Tom Kempinski
Director   Andrei Konchalovsky
Producers   Menahem Golan
                                         Yoram Globus
Screenplay   Tom Kempinski
                                         Jeremy Lipp
                                         Andrei Konchalovsky
Camera (Rank color)   Alex Thomson
Editor   Henry Richardson
Orchestrations   Michael Linn
Soloist   Nigel Kennedy
Designer   John Graysmark
Set Decorator   Peter Young
Art Directors   Reg Bream
                                         Steve Cooper
Sound (Dolby)   David Crozier
Costumes   Evangeline Harrison
Assistant Director   David Tringham
Associate Producer   Michael J. Kagan
Casting   Noel Davis
                                         Jeremy Zimmerman

<u>Cast</u>
Stephanie Anderson   Julie Andrews
David Cornwallis   Alan Bates
Dr. Louis Feldman   Max Von Sydow
Constantine Kassanis   Rupert Everett
Sonia Randovich   Margaret Courtenay
Penny Smallwood   Cathryn Harrison
Leonid Lefimov   Sigfrit Steiner
Totter   Liam Neeson
Anys   Macha Meril
Mrs. Burridge   Janette Newling
Drunk   John Delaney
Derek   Kevin Ranson
Betty   Dorothea Philips
Gail   Marcia Linden
Charlie   David Miller
Terry   Gary Fairhall
Joan   Nicola Davies
Woman in Pub   Pam Brighton
Betsy   Nicola Perring

<u>Synopsis</u>
     At the urging of her husband (a composer), Stephanie Anderson, an
internationally acclaimed concert violinist, decides to visit a psychiartrist, Dr. Louis

Feldman. In her first visit, Stephanie breaks the well kept secret that she is suffering from multiple sclerosis.

Most of those around her (her husband, her agent, Sonia, and her pianist, Leonid, try to gloss over the fact that her days as a performer are numbered. But her pupil, Constantin, insists on bringing reality to the surface.

Stephanie suffers a nightmare in which she breaks down on the concert stage and must be carried off. She opts to accept a number of recording engagements and cancels her next major public appearance in concert.

Shortly thereafter, she discovers that her husband is having an affair with his secretary. In a desperate move, she begins a passionate affair with a delivery man, but eventually feels guilty because he is married, and decides to end the relationship.

She is subsequently rescued from a suicide attempt. After a year has passed, she invites her husband David and her prize ex-pupil Constantin to a birthday party. She has learned to cope with the fact that neither is any longer an intimate part of her life. She leaves the party and seeks solitude visiting an old oak tree that has apparently been a source of strength in her life. She finally appears to have accepted the unthinkable and make peace with herself.

Commentary

Duet For One presented Julie at the absolute peak of her abilities as a dramatic actress. She gave a nearly flawless performance in a flawed film. Unfortunately, the film had little impact on her career. Half-heartedly released by a financially troubled Cannon Films to a limited art house audience, the film had very little exposure. In 1986, Julie was heavily promoted in some circles for an Oscar nomination for either this role or *That's Life!* (or both), but neither film had much of a profile and both were apparently brushed aside in the minds of voting Academy members.

Reviewers generally conceded that Julie was much better than the film itself. She was light years away from *Mary Poppins* here in a three-dimensional portrait of a dying woman learning to accept the things she cannot change. She handled scenes of anger, bitterness, despair, courage, sweetness, and sexual fervor with finesse.

Based on a two-character play by Tom Kempenski, the attempts to open the material up for film apparently diluted too much of the dramatic impact. Not really dull, but also not gripping, the film ambles along from scene to scene in search of a cohesive filmic style. Worse yet, it comes across as preachy and simplistic at times. If it weren't for its decidely British stiff upper lip atmosphere, it might resemble a made-for-TV disease-of-the-week movie.

It is, however, quite well acted. Rupert Everett was alternately touching and contemptible as Stephanie's prize pupil Constantin, who makes those around him confront the reality of what's happening to Stephanie. Alan Bates is appropriately unsympathetic as her philandering husband. Max von Sydow (Julie's costar in *Hawaii*) is very good, as usual, in the ancillary role as Stephanie's psychiatrist.

The film was such a personal triumph for Julie that it's a shame it hasn't led to more challenging and compelling roles for her.

Reviews

Variety (12/31/86) -- *Variety* had a mixed reaction to this film, which was typical of most other appraisals. The reviewer felt that when the film focused closely on the characters, it was "a moving portrait of life in turmoil." However, the film was said to "degenerate into saccharine platitudes" when director Andre Konchalovsky "shoots for big statements." The early portions of the film were seen to be stronger, as the world of classical music was carefully depicted. The film was said to be "full of lovely musical interludes." Alan Bates as the philandering husband made a strong impression on the reviewer, as did Max Von Sydow as "a cold Freudian with a soft heart." The film was said to present the subject of therapy "with the solemnity of a summit conference." Little mention was made of Julie's performance, except for her adeptness in believably pretending to play a violin.

New York Times (2/14/87) -- The *Times* found that "for all its sogginess and contrivance," *Duet* came across as a "compelling vehicle, particularly for a star who fits the material as well as Julie Andrews does." The reviewer made the point that in *That's Life!* -- and especially in this film -- Julie was being allowed to "draw upon previously underused aspects of her talent." In *Duet*, the reviewer found Julie's acting to be considerably better than the material itself (which was another point many reviewers had made about *That's Life!*). Rupert Everett was seen as the only other cast member besides Julie to deliver an impressive performance.

Stage Appearances

This chapter is divided into three parts. For indexing purposes, however, each entry in the chapter is numbered consecutively regardless of section divisions, beginning with **S01** in the first section. Following are the three sections:

THE EARLY YEARS chronicles Julie's live appearances as actress or singer in England prior to her first U.S. appearance in *The Boy Friend* (1954)

THE BROADWAY YEARS covers the period between 1954-1962, when Julie appeared in *The Boy Friend, My Fair Lady,* and *Camelot.*

HOLLYWOOD AND BEYOND covers the years between 1962 and the present. Julie's stage credits in this period include concerts and other live personal appearances, but no plays or musicals.

| THE EARLY YEARS |

S01 *Stage Door Canteen* (Picadilly, London; December 5, 1946)
Julie (age 11) sang "Polonaise" from *Mignon* and "When I Sing" (from
Tchaikovski's *Sleeping Beauty*). After the performance, Julie was introduced
to the Queen Mother and Princess Margaret.

S02 *Starlight Roof Revue* (London Hippodrome; Opened October 23, 1947)
Julie (at age 12) sang "I Am Titania" and "Polonaise" from *Mignon*.

S03 *Royal Command Performance* (London Palladium; November 1, 1948)
Julie became the youngest solo performer ever selected to appear before
royalty at the Palladium. Attending: King George VI, Queen Elizabeth (later
Queen Mother), Princess Elizabeth (later Queen Elizabeth), and Princess
Margaret.

S04 *Aladdin* and *Humpty Dumpty* (London Casino; Christmas 1948 through March
5, 1949)
Julie played Princess Balroulbadour in *Aladdin* and the egg in Humpty
Dumpty. She first met her future husband, Tony Walton, here.

S05 *Concert Appearance* (Coconut Grove and Hippodrome in Blackpool,
England; July, 1949)
During this singing engagement, Julie's parents, Ted and Barbara Andrews,
were appearing in *The Orchid Room* at Central Pier, Blackpool.

S06 *Concert Appearance* (Winter Gardens, Margate; July 17-21, 1950).

S07 *Little Red Riding Hood* (Theatre Royal,Nottingham; Christmas, 1950)
Julie played the title role and sang "Waltz Song."

S08 *Concert Appearance* (Garrick Theatre, Southport, Yorkshire; May, 1951)
Julie sang, with Barbara Andrews at the piano. She was billed as "the
phenomenal juvenile singing star."

S09 *Concert Appearance* (Manchester Hippodrome, Manchester; June 11-16,
1951).

S10 *Look In* revue (Palace Varieties, Blackpool; April, 1952).

S11 *Jack and the Beanstock* (Hippodrome Theatre, Coventry; December 23, 1952)
Julie appeared as Princess Bettina.

S12 *Cap and Belles tour* (Empire Theatre in Nottingham; also in Glasgow and
Scotland, among other locales; 1953).

S13 *Cinderella* by Michael Bishop, Eric Sykes, and Spike Milligan (London
Palladium; opened December 24, 1953)
Julie played the title role (which she would again play in 1957 in the Rodgers
and Hammerstein TV version -- see **T03**). Directed by Val Parnell.
Additional dialogue and numbers by Phil Pork. Decor: Charles Reading.
Ballets arranged by Pauline Grant and staged by Charles Henry. Cast:
William Barrett, Edna Russe, Casavecchia Troupe, Joan Mann, David Dale,
Ted and George Durante, Richard Hearne, Max Bygraves, and Cyril Wells.

S14 *Mountain Fire* tour (Royal Court, Liverpool; May 18 - August, 1954)
Also played in the Grand Theatre, Leeds, Yorkshire, and the Theatre Royal in
Birmingham. Julie played a Southern belle, Betty Dunbar, in a
dramatic performance. The play was an American drama with music written
by Howard Richardson and William Bearney. It was severely pounced by the
critics and never made its way to London, as had been planned. Julie
remained friends with William Bearney, whom she dated in New York during
the Broadway runs of *The Boy Friend* and *My Fair Lady*.

THE BROADWAY YEARS

S15　　　　　*THE BOY FRIEND* (1954)

Credits

Book, Music, Lyrics	Sandy Wilson
Producers	Cy Feuer
	Ernest Martin
Director	Vida Hope
Choreographer	John Heawood
Sets/Costumes	Reginald Wooley
Orchestra	Paul McGrane and His
	Bearcats
Musical Director	Anton Coppola
Orchestrations	Ted Royal
	Charles R. Cooke
Stage Managers	Charles Pratt, Jr.
	David Kanter
	Marge Ellis
Company Manager	Michael Goldreyer
Scenery/Lighting Supervision	Feder
Costume Supervision	Robert Mackintosh
Press	Karl Bernstein
	Harvey Sabinson
	Robert Ganshaw

Cast

Hortense	Paulette Girard
Nancy	Millicent Martin
Maisie	Ann Wakefield
Fay	Stella Claire
Dulcie	Dilya Lay
Polly	Julie Andrews
Marcel	Joe Milan
Alphouse	Buddy Schwab
Pierre	Jerry Newby
Madame Dubonnet	Ruth Altman
Bobby Van Heusen	Bob Scheerer
Percival Brown	Eric Berry
Tony	John Hewer
Phillipe	Jimmy Alex
Monica	Berkely Marsh
Lord Brockhurst	Geoffrey Hibbert
Lady Brockhurst	Moyna MacGill
	Susanne Lynne Connorty
Guests	Phoebe Mackay
	Marge Ellis
	Mickey Calin
Gendarme	Douglas Deane
Waiter	Lyn Robert
Pepe	Joe Milan
Lolita	Stella Claire

Understudies: Polly, Ann Wakefield; Tony, Douglas Deane; Maisie and Fay, Millicent Martin; Bobby, Jerry Newby; Mme. Dubonnet, Rose Inghram; Percival, Leonard Ceeley; Lady Brockhurst, Phoebe Mackay; Lord Brockhurst, Walter Burke; Hortense, Marge Ellis; Dulcie, Stella Claire; Nancy, Lyn Connorty; Marcel, Buddy Schwab; Pierre and Alphonse, Jimmy Alex.

The Play's History

The Boy Friend opened January 14, 1954 at Wyndham's Theatre in London (not starring Julie). It ran for 2084 performances.

It was first performed on Broadway at the Royale Theatre, September 30, 1954, starring Julie in her U.S. stage debut. It ran for 485 performances.

It was revived in London on November 29, 1967 (without Julie) at the Comedy Theatre. It ran for 367 performances.

It was revived on Broadway at the Ambassador Theatre (without Julie) on April 14, 1979. It ran for 119 performances

In the mid-60s, producer Ross Hunter tried unsuccessfully to acquire the rights to *The Boy Friend* from MGM (who had previously purchased them). Hunter wanted the property as a movie musical vehicle for Julie Andrews. MGM eventually hired controversial-but-hot director Ken Russell (*Women in Love, Tommy, Altered States*) to helm the project. In his usual eccentric style, Russell fashioned a film that was less a musical entertainment than it was an avant garde art house film. Russell cast fashion model Twiggy in her American film debut in Julie's role (Polly). Despite Russell's heavyhanded stylistic touches, the film was not without its charming and hilarious moments. It is sort of a cult favorite, and was recently restored in its original full-length version.

Synopsis

The year is 1926. The place is Madame Dubonnet's finishing school at the Villa Caprice on the outskirts of Nice, France. The Perfect Young Ladies who attend Madame's school all share one vital objective: to find that one irreplaceable, absolutely essential item -- a boy friend.

Charming young heiress Polly Browne is no exception. But how does a poor little rich girl find a boy who wants her for herself -- not for her money? This question is put to the test when Polly meets a handsome young messenger boy, Tony. Although romance is clearly in the air, the love affair will have to weather a series of complications before the inevitable happy ending.

Other romantic subplots span the generations, such as the autumnal attraction between Madame Dubonnet and Polly's father, Percival. But the real burning question centers on Polly and Tony. When will love conquer all?

The answer comes in the happy conclusion, when it's revealed that Tony is not really a penniless member of the working class. He is actually the son of Lord and Lady Brockhurst, who has been in search of a girl who wants him for himself -- not for his money. So Polly and Tony will be united after all, settling down in the charming little room in Bloomsbury that heretofore they could only croon about.

See the *Discography* section **(D02)** for a complete list of musical numbers.

Commentary

Julie made her U.S. stage debut in this featherweight pastiche of the Roaring 20s musicals. She had not starred in the show in England, where it premiered, but was tapped for the lead role of Polly when a version was mounted for Broadway importation.

Though light in content and modest in ambitions, the Sandy Wilson musical has enhanced its reputation over the years, due to its near-perfect amalgamation of book, music, and lyrics into an artfully assembled and completely cohesive piece of musical theatre. It still holds up today as a pleasant, toe-tapping entertainment. It remains a favorite of college and community theatre productions, as it provides excellent experience for young performers to try their hand at broad, stylized acting. Curiously, the enormously talented author/lyricist Wilson never had another hit.

Although it's more an ensemble piece than a star vehicle, Julie stood out in the romantic female lead role of Polly, a demure flapper hoping to win the heart of her beloved Tony. Most reviews singled her out as especially outstanding in a polished and thoroughly enjoyable production.

The role was not strong enough to catapult Julie to instant stardom, but it certainly opened the right doors, leading to her audition for the lead female role, Eliza Doolittle, in the much more demanding and ambitious musical *My Fair Lady*.

Julie clearly called upon her experience with this show when she acted in the film *Thoroughly Modern Millie* more than 20 years later, although by then she was a more seasoned, mature performer. Nevertheless, this was an excellent vehicle for Julie's introduction to U.S. audiences.

Reviews
New York Times (10/1/54) -- Calling this show "a delightful burlesque," the *Times* reviewer had difficulty deciding which was funnier: "the material or the performances." The staging was termed "superb." Yet the review singled out Julie, in the role of the heroine, Polly Browne, as the probable reason for the show's "special quality." Her performance was said to have more than irony. Her "romantic sadness" was said to sometimes come across as "almost moving."

*****

S16   *MY FAIR LADY* (1956)

Credits
Adapted from George Bernard Shaw's play *Pygmalion*

Book and Lyrics	Alan Jay Lerner
Music	Frederick Loewe
Director	Moss Hart
Choreographer	Hanya Holm
Designer	Oliver Smith
Costumes	Cecil Beaton
Musical Arrangements	Rupert Russell Bennet
	Phil Lang
Lighting	Feder
Dance Music Arrangements	Trude Rittman
Musical Director	Franz Allers
Stage Managers	Samuel Liff
	Jerry Adler
	Bernard Hart
General Manager	Philip Adler
Press	Richard Maney
	Peggy Phillips
	Robert Hector
	Martin Schwartz

Cast

Buskers	Imelda De Martin
	Cal Jeffrey
	Joe Rocco
Mrs. Eynsford-Hill	Viola Roche
Eliza Doolittle	Julie Andrews
Freddy Eynsford-Hill	John Michael King
Colonel Pickering	Robert Coote
Bystander	Christopher Hewett
Henry Higgins	Rex Harrison
Selsey Man	Gordon Dilworth
Hoxton Man	David Thomas
First Cockney	Reid Shelton
Second Cockney	Glenn Lezer
Third Cockney	James Morris
Fourth Cockney	Herb Surface
Bartender	David Thomas
Harry	George Dilworth
Jamie	Rod McLennan
Alfred P. Doolittle	Stanley Holloway
Mrs. Pearce	Philippa Bevans
Mrs. Hopkins	Olive Reeves-Smith
Butler	Reid Shelton
Servants	Rosemary Gaines
	Collen O'Connor
	Muriel Shaw
	Gloria Van Dorpe
	Glenn Kezer
Mrs. Higgins	Cathleen Nesbitt
Chauffer	Barton Mumaw
Footmen	Gordon Ewing
	William Krach
Lord Boxington	Gordon Dilworth
Lady Boxington	Olive Reeves-Smith
Constable	Barton Mumaw
Flower Girl	Cathy Conklin
Zoltan Karpathy	Christopher Hewett
Flunkey	Paul Brown
Queen of Transylvania	Maribel Hammer
Ambassador	Rod McLennan
Bartender	Paul Brown
Mrs. Higgins' Maid	Judith Williams

Singing Ensemble: Melisande Congdon, Lola Fisher, Rosemary Gaines, Maribel Hammer, Colleen O'Connor, Muriel Shaw, Patti Spangler, Gloria Van Dorpe, Paul Brown, Gordon Ewing, Glenn Kezer, William Krach, James Morris, Reid Shelton, Herb Surface, David Thomas

Dancing Ensemble: Estelle Aza, Cathy Conklin, Imelda De Martin, Pat Diamond, Pat Drylie, Barbara Heath, Vera Lee, Nancy Lynch, Judith Williams, Thatcher Clarke, Crandall Diehl, David Evans, Carl Jeffrey, Barton Mumaw, Gene Nettles, Paul Olson, Joe Rocco, Fernando Schaffenburg, James White

Understudies: Higgins, Christopher Hewett; Eliza, Constance Brigham; Doolittle, Gordon Dilworth; Mrs.Higgins, Viola Roche; Pickering, Rod McLennan; Freddy, Reid Shelton; Mrs. Pearce and Mrs. Eynsford-Hill, Olive Reeves-Smith; Karpathy, David Thomas; Jamie, Paul Brown; Harry, Glenn Kezer; Mrs. Hopkins, Maribel Hammer

The Play's History

The play premiered on Broadway starring Julie at the Mark Hellinger Theatre on March 15, 1956. It ran for 2717 performances.

It's London premiere (also with Julie) opened April 30, 1958, at the Drury Lane Theatre. It ran for 2281 performances)

The first Broadway revival (without Julie) opened March 25, 1976, at the St. James Theatre. It ran for 384 performances

The first London revival (also without Julie) opened October 25, 1979 at the Adelphi Theatre. It ran for 847 performances

Though diehard Julie Andrews fans may have to choke to admit it, *My Fair Lady* became an almost flawless movie musical, one of the handful of truly great film musicals to have come out since the 50s. Audrey Hepburn gave a brilliant performance in the role created by Julie, and Rex Harrison triumphantly repeated his stage *tour de force* as Professor Higgins. George Cukor's impeccable direction was extremely faithful to the stage *My Fair Lady*, without seeming stale.

Synopsis

The famous *My Fair Lady* storyline, very closely adapted from its source material (George Bernard Shaw's *Pygmalion*), is a rags-to-riches story that has been imitated in literary works time and time again, due to its timeless and moving portrait of the human condition.

Professor Harold Higgins, England's most renowned professor of dialects and speech, makes a boast to his distinguished friend, Colonel Pickering. Within six weeks, he will transform a downtrodden Cockney flower girl into an articulate and well-bred lady -- or, at least, he will be able to pass her off as such. Pickering challenges him on the bet.

The pawn in the wager is spunky Eliza Doolittle, who makes a meager wage selling flowers on the street. Her father is n'er-do-well Alfred P. Doolittle, who spends his days with his cronies drinking ale in the pubs. Eliza allows herself to be a part of the gambit because she wants to learn proper speech, assuming that will elevate her stature in England's rigid class structure, and eventually allow her to become a businesswoman.

It's immediately apparent that Higgins is using Eliza as a mere instrument in his self-serving game and has little interest in the girl's feelings. He drills her day and night, and shows virtually no consideration for her well being and happiness. Teaching Eliza is a long and difficult task, and things look quite discouraging until one night when she perfectly recites his "Rain in Spain" lesson with impeccable diction. This gives Eliza the encouragement she needs to go all the way and make good on the wager.

Higgins and Pickering decide to give Eliza a trial run by taking her to the horse races at Ascot. Eliza's diction is flawless, but her topics of conversation stray considerably from what is considered proper in British society circles. Though this is seemingly a terrible setback, Higgins ignores Pickering's pleading for the bet to be called off. He proceeds with his plans to show Eliza off at the Embassy Ball.

After a hair-raising evening at the ball, Higgins is delighted to announce that Eliza did even better than anyone had dreamed. The rumor at the ball was that she was secretly a Hungarian princess. Higgins and Pickering pat each other on the back and celebrate triumphantly, while poor Eliza is completely overlooked. No one recognizes the credit she deserves for such a splendid success, nor her need to join in on the celebration.

After a bitter fight with Higgins, Eliza leaves the household and goes to Higgins' kindly mother for consolation. She has a lovestruck suitor in young Freddy Eynsford-Hill, but she has a special affection for Higgins that is really foremost in her mind. Her need to be treated like a lady by him seems to be the ultimate test for her to know she has truly become a person of worth.

Higgins finally locates the "missing" Eliza at his mother's house, where Eliza delights in really telling him off, then departing, saying she never intends to see him again. Higgins sulks to his mother, then decides to go home. But on the way, he comes to realize that he does have an affection for her. This is in the humblest moment in the play for such an egocentric man. He's grown accustomed to her face and wonders how he's going to get along without seeing it again.

In a departure from Shaw's original play, Eliza returns at the end and we are to assume that she and Higgins will at least settle on some level of mutual communication. It may or may not be romance, but if nothing else if would seem to be some form of satisfactory respect for Eliza. She has finally become a genuine lady in more than simply her speech delivery, and she deserves to be treated as such.

See the *Discography* section **(D03)** for a complete list of musical numbers.

Commentary

As Broadway legends and movie musical lore go, it's hard to find anything to surpass the luster of *My Fair Lady*. The melding of a great play (George Bernard Shaw's *Pygmalion*) with an incomparable musical score (Alan Jay Lerner, lyrics; Frederick Loewe, music) alone was enough to secure the show a place in the top ranks of American musical comedy. In its 1956 premiere production on Broadway, the masterful staging of Moss Hart and the brilliance of the cast (Julie, Rex Harrison, Stanley Holloway, Cathleen Nesbitt) made *My Fair Lady* a legend in its own time. It was an instant classic.

Aside from the skillful way that Lerner and Loewe seamlessly wove beautiful music and completely appropriate lyrics into the fabric of Shaw's intelligent comedy-drama, the real beauty of the show was the way it made literate, thought-provoking theatre out of the musical comedy form. Others have tried and failed to make musicals out of classic drama (such as *Dear World*, the musicalization of *The Madwoman of Chaillot*), and others have succeeded in such adaptations by making radical changes from the original source material (i.e. *West Side Story* from *Shakespeare's Romeo and Juliet*). But never before had a musical been created that essentially left the original text intact, simply embellishing it with appropriate music. What a glorious way to make dramatic classics palatable as popular entertainment.

In her biggest acting challenge up to that time, Julie, became an American stage star of the first degree, thanks to her impeccable voice, charming stage presence, and multi-leveled characterization. The fact that she was to do only one more Broadway musical after *Lady* (*Camelot* in 1960) seems a shame. Hollywood simply snatched her up too quickly. It would be a delight to have Julie return to Broadway in an appropriate vehicle, but all discussions that begin that way (such as a stage musical based on *Victor/Victoria* and a revival of the Gershwin/Weill *Lady in the Dark*) never seem to materialize. It's easy to imagine Julie in a revival of *A Little Night Music*, perhaps, or another classy vehicle befitting her stature. Or better yet, how about a new Stephen Sondheim musical tailored especially for Julie?

Julie had her share of frustrations in preparing the role, not the least of which was the script's incredibly difficult task of evolving from a coarse, street-bred, slurring Cockney flower girl into a charming and cultured lady with perfect diction and glamour to spare. Prior to this part, Julie had not been given particularly challenging roles on the English stage or in her Broadway debut as the ingenue Polly in *The Boy Friend*. Hart clearly took a gamble in casting her in such a demanding lead role.

As Julie related on a March, 1988 PBS-TV special saluting the talents of Lerner and Loewe (see **T52**), she was having such a difficult time mastering the part that she expected to be shipped back to England. However, Hart decided to take the bull by the horns, drilling her nonstop for an entire weekend, going over the role again and again until she began to offer an interpretation that was on the right track. Apparently the weekend worked as planned, because Julie stayed with the show and went on to receive endless accolades, including a Tony nomination.

The big scandal connected with the show, of course, is the uproar in Hollywood when Jack Warner passed up Julie in favor of Audrey Hepburn for the 1964 screen version of *My Fair Lady*. The controversy escalated when Audrey was completely overlooked in the Best Actress Oscar nominations, while Julie waltzed away with the big prize that very same year for her film debut in *Mary Poppins*. Throughout the years, Julie has often said that she never really expected to get the role because she was a newcomer to this country without a Hollywood boxoffice track record. But she surely must have been disappointed.

After playing the role on Broadway for more than a year, Julie took some time off, then dusted off her bouqet of flowers to resume the role in London in April, 1958, with Rex Harrison and the other principal players also repeating their roles. Predictably, it was almost as big a hit in England as it was in the U.S. (It was surely one of the most English-accented shows ever imported from Broadway to London, rather than the other way around.)

In subsequent years, Rex Harrison has appeared in revivals of the show, but Julie has resisted that temptation, and of course, eventually grew too old to even consider it.

Reviews

New York Times (3/16/56) -- Setting the pace for the glowing reviews to follow, the *Times* called *Lady* "a wonderful show." Rex Harrison and Julie were praised for playing their roles with "the light, dry touch of top-flight Shavian acting." The duo's perfomances were said to make the show "affecting as well as amusing." Julie's acting was called "triumphant." Harrison was found to be "perfect." The reviewer felt that the show added qualities to the "agile intelligence" of Shaw's writing: "the warmth, loveliness, and excitement of a memorable theatre frolic."

*****

S17   *CAMELOT* (1960)

Credits

Based on the book *The Once and Future King* by T.H. White

Book and Lyrics	Alan Jay Lerner
Music	Frederick Loewe
Director	Moss Hart
Producers	Alan Jay Lerner
	Frederick Loewe
	Moss Hart
Designer	Oliver Smith
Choreography	Hanya Holm
Costumes	Adrian Duquette
	Tony Duquette
Lighting	Feder
Musical Director	Franz Allers
Orchestrations	Robert Russell Bennett
	Philip J. Lang
Dance/Choral Arrangements	Trude Rittman
Hair Styles	Ernest Adler
Production Stage Manager	Robert Downing
Stage Managers	Edward Preston
	Bernard Hart
	Jonathan Anderson
Press	Richard Maney
	Martin Schwartz

Cast

Sir Dinadin	John Cullum
Sir Lionel	Bruce Yarnell
Merlyn	David Hurst
Arthur	Richard Burton
Guenevere	Julie Andrews
Nimue	Marjorie Smith
Page	Leland Mayforth
Lancelot	Robert Goulet
Dap	Michael Clarke-Laurence
Pellinore	Robert Coote
Clarius	Richard Kuch
Lady Anne	Christina Gillespie
Lady	Leesa Troy
Sir Sagramore	James Gannon
Page	Peter De Vise
Herald	John Starkweather
Lady Catherine	Virginia Allen
Modred	Roddy McDowall
Sir Oranna	Michael Kermoyan
Sir Gwilliam	Jack Dabdoub
Morgan Le Fey	M'el Dowd
Tom	Robin Stewart

Singing Ensemble: Joan August, Mary Sue Berry, Marnell Bruce, Judy Hastings, Benita James, Marjorie Smith, Sheila Swenson, Leesa Troy, Dorothy White, Frank Bouley, Jack Dabdoub, James Gannon, Murray Goldkind, Warren Hays, Paul Huddleston, Michael Kermoyan, David Maloof, Larry Mitchell, Paul Richards, John Taliaferro

Dancing Ensemble: Virginia Allen, Judi Allinson, Laurie Archer, Carlene Carroll, Joan Coddington, Katia Geleznova, Adriana Keathley, Dawn Mitchell, Claudia Schroeder, Beti Seay, Jerry Bowers, Peter Deign, Randy Doney, Richard Englund, Richard Gain, Gene GeBauer, James Kirby, Richard Kuch, Joe Nelson, John Starkweather, Jimmy Tarbutton

The Play's History

The play premiered on Broadway (starring Julie) on December 3, 1960, at the Majestic Theatre. It ran for 873 performances

Its London premiere (without Julie) was August 19, 1964, at the Drury Lane Theatre. It ran for 518 performances

Its Broadway revival (without Julie) opened November 15, 1981 at the Winter Garden Theatre. It ran for 48 performances.

Vanessa Redgrave, Richard Harris, and Franco Nero (not a boxoffice star or singer among them) inherited the movie throne from Julie, Richard Burton, and Robert Goulet, respectively. *Camelot* was a flawed, sometimes lumbering film, adding to the ongoing parade of botched stage-to-film transplants by director Joshua Logan, (*South Pacific, Paint Your Wagon*). But the strong acting of the stars still made for an affecting, memorable experience.

Synopsis

The rich legend of King Arthur and his Knights of the Round Table and a book by T. H. White were the source materials for this ambitious musical.

A frightened King Arthur and a defiant Guenevere are betrothed to marry each other sight unseen. As Guenevere attempts to run away on her wedding day, she literally stumbles onto her future husband. After an awkward introduction, Arthur and Guenevere warm up to each other and are thereafter married.

In the kingdom of Camelot, where Arthur and Guenevere reign, Arthur devises an improved order of chivalry, based on new concepts that ban senseless violence and advocate respect for one's fellow man. He conceives of the Round Table, so that all knights will have equal authority and none will sit at the head of the table and feel they are in command.

Frequently consulting with his mentor, Merlin the Magician, Arthur carries out his noble ambitions, turning Camelot into an idyllic kingdom of respect and peacefulness, heralded throughout the world.

From France comes heroic Lancelot du Lac to join the king's order. Guenevere is initially turned off by this boastful, almost too good to be true creature, but Arthur is impressed and quickly beknights him.

Before anyone realizes what's happening, Guenevere and Lancelot are falling in love with each other. Their love is secret for a long time, but is eventually too much to bear. They give in to their passions, violating the chivalric order of the day.

Arthur tries to deny what he sees before his eyes. Not only will he suffer the pain of losing the love of his life and his dearest friend. He knows that if the truth ever comes out, it will be the end of his flawless regime in Camelot.

His bitter illegitimate son, Modred, enters the picture and does not allow Arthur to deny the truth any longer. The truth comes out. Dissension and fighting return to Camelot. Lancelot flees capture, but Guenevere is kept in captivity and sentenced to burn at the stake for treason. At the last possible moment, Lancelot arrives ands rescues Guenevere.

War intensifies in Camelot and the Round table is soon a thing of the past. King Arthur and his chivalric order are finished.

Arthur eventually has a reunion with a tearful Guenevere, who has joined the religious order of Holy Sisters. As Guenvere departs, Arthur seems destined for a life of endless regret and despair, until a young lad, Tom of Warwick, stumbles onto the battlefield.

Tom speaks with wonderment and great respect of Arthur, Camelot, and the Round Table, not realizing that the era is over. Arthur realizes that he has made an imprint on history with Camelot. He feels what he achieved will not be forgotten. Perhaps sometime in history there will be a peaceful, just land as cherished as Camelot. If Camelot is remembered, there is always hope that it will resurface.

See the *Discography* section **(D11)** for a complete list of musical numbers.

Commentary

Camelot, the King Arthur musical, is more appreciated today than it was when it premiered at the beginning of the 60s. Though *Camelot's* initial reception was lukewarm at best, it is one of the most fondly remembered American musicals for three primary reasons: 1) Its connection to the John F. Kennedy legend ("Don't let it be forgot..."); 2) its casting of superstars-to-be (Richard Burton, Julie, Robert Goulet) before they hit their prime, and 3) its continuing popularity as a sort of cult movie musical.

Camelot was no *My Fair Lady*, though it was assembled by most of the same creative team, from director Moss Hart to composers Lerner and Loewe to star Julie. But that's an unfair comparison. In its own right, *Camelot* was a captivating, if overlong, evening of theatre. The mammoth production values sometimes outweighed what was essentially a triangular love story between King Arthur (Burton), his Queen Guenevere (Julie), and Sir Lancelot (Goulet).

But that may indicate another problem. Is adultery an appropriate central plot for a Broadway musical? In 1960, perhaps not. Today, after *Sweeney Todd* (about a murderous barber) and *Les Miserables* (social drama based on a classic French novel), not to mention *West Side Story* (street gang warfare), most any topic seems fair game. At the time, though, the show may have seemed too downbeat. Kitty

Carlisle, Moss Hart's widow, seems to think so, having made that assertion when she was interviewed in the March 1988 documentary special on Lerner and Loewe that aired on PBS-TV (see **T52**).

Camelot combined a swashbuckling romantic adventure with an optimistic *Man of La Mancha* type of theme into a musical that sometimes veered close to operetta in execution. Lerner and Loewe's melodies were among their very finest, including gorgeous ballads ("If Ever I Would Leave You," "I Loved You Once in Silence"), *My Fair Lady* type solliloquies ("I Wonder What the King is Doing Tonight," "The Simple Joys of Maidenhood"), comic numbers ("Fie On Goodness," "Take Me to the Fair"), and traditional Broadway uplift ("Camelot").

Camelot had legendary problems on the road. Goulet was nearly fired. Hart suffered a heart attack. Lerner had physical ails. And audience responses were lukewarm. The show was tinkered with right up until opening night. It enjoyed a huge advance sale on the strength of the names of the stars and of Lerner and Loewe. But the producers still feared it may not last long once the advance sales began to play out.

The play opened on Broadway in December, 1960, to mixed reviews -- few outright pans but also few unqualified endorsements. According to Robert Goulet in the PBS Lerner and Loewe special, it wasn't until the cast appeared on Ed Sullivan's show in March, 1960, performing numbers from the show, that the boxoffice began to improve. The show finally developed into a bona fide, if hardly record-breaking Broadway hit.

Julie, as usual, walked away with pristine notices. The role was obviously not as flamboyant as Eliza Dolittle in *My Fair Lady*, but it was challenging and different from her previous roles. She more than met the challenge.

The show didn't open in London until 1964. None of the principal Broadway cast repeated their roles. Although Burton appeared in a revival of the show in the 1980s until he had to drop out with back trouble, Julie never repeated the role. She reportedly had some discussions with Jack Warner (again) about appearing in the 1967 film version, but their deal never came to fruition.

Reviews

New York Times (12/5/60) -- Though admiring its pleasant-looking performers and beautiful vistas, the *Times* termed *Camelot* "a partly enchanted city." Julie, said to come across as a "slim, airy person," was found to be lovely as both actress and singer, and her character Guenevere to be "regal and girlish, cool and eager." Richard Burton and Julie were praised for their "winning lightness" of performing. The *Times* reviewer felt that *Camelot* was weighed down by its book, terming the style of story-telling "inconsistent" and much of the humor "obvious." Though Robert Goulet was praised for his acting and singing in the role of Lancelot, the character was thought to be "a crashing bore." The score was admired for Alan Jay Lerner's "clever" lyrics and Frederick Loewe's "pleasant" tunes. The overall show was said to "lean dangerously in the direction of old-hat operetta."

New York Mirror (12/5/60) -- The *Mirror* was also impressed with the show's "pageantry and spectacle" but felt that *Camelot* was "no *My Fair Lady*." The musical score was found to be "just fair." All in all, *Camelot* was "an expensive disappointment" to the *Mirror's* reviewer.

New York World-Telegram (12/5/60) -- This paper delivered one of the production's few unqualified raves. The reviewer claimed to "sit in open-mouthed wonder at the uninhibited splendor." Julie was called "ravishing." Richard Burton was said to be "immensely likable." The show was said to possess "gayety and grandeur" and "almost unbelievable" beauty.

HOLLYWOOD AND BEYOND

S18   *Julie and Carol at Carnegie Hall.* Carnegie Hall, New York. June 11, 1962 (single performance; taped for CBS-TV special). See *Discography* **(D14)** for a complete list of musical numbers and *Television Appearances* **(T11)** for more details on the television special.

S19   *Academy Awards 1964.* Santa Monica Civic Auditorium. Santa Monica, CA. 4/13/64 (broadcast live over ABC-TV). Appearing at the Academy Awards for the first time, Julie presented the Best Foreign Film award to Federico Fellini for *8 1/2*. She did not make her film debut until September of that year (*Mary Poppins*). For more details, see *Television Appearances* **(T12)**.

S20   *Academy Awards 1965.* Santa Monica Civic Auditorium. Santa Monica, CA. 4/5/65 (broadcast live over ABC-TV). Julie won the Best Actress Oscar for *Mary Poppins* and appeared to accept it. For more details, see *Television Appearances* **(T15)**.

S21   *Academy Awards 1966.* Santa Monica Civic Auditorium. Santa Monica, CA. 4/18/66 (broadcast live over ABC-TV). Julie appeared as a nominee for Best Actress in *The Sound of Music*, but lost to Julie Christie (*Darling*). She also presented the Best Actor Oscar to Lee Marvin (*Cat Ballou*), and accepted the Best Director award for an absent Robert Wise (*The Sound of Music*). For more details, see *Television Appearances* **(T16)**.

S22   *Academy Awards 1968.* Santa Monica Civic Auditorium. Santa Monica, CA. 4/10/68 (broadcast live over ABC-TV). Julie appeared to present the Best Picture award for *In the Heat of the Night* to producer Walter Mirisch. For more details, see *Television Appearances* **(T17)**.

S23   *Tony Awards.* New York. 6/6/70. Julie appeared as co-hostess for this live telecast.

S24   *Emmy Awards.* New York. 5/14/72. Julie appeared to accept an award for Glenda Jackson.

S25   *Julie and Carol at Lincoln Center.* Lincoln Center, New York. July 1, 1972 (single performance; taped for CBS-TV special). See *Discography* **(D26)** for a complete list of musical numbers and *Television Appearances* **(T24)** for more details on the television special.

S26   *Academy Awards 1973.* Santa Monica Civic Auditorium. Santa Monica, CA. 4/5/65 (broadcast live over ABC-TV). Julie appeared to present the Best Director award to Bob Fossee (*Cabaret*), along with George Stevens. For more details, see *Television Appearances* **(T29)**.

S27   *Christmas Concert*. Royal Albert Hall, London. December 4, 1973.
Julie sang Christmas carols with the London Symphony Orchestra, conducted by
Andre Previn.

S28   *British Screen Awards*. London. 3/6/74. Julie appeared to present an
acting award to Walter Matthau.

S29   *Philharmonic 1974*. Royal Albert Hall, London. 10/26/74. Julie
introduced the Philharmonic on the occasion of their 1974 season.

S30   *Salute to Sir Lew Grade*. New York Hilton. 4/18/75. Julie and Tom
Jones sang in this musical tribute to Producer Lew Grade (who produced Julie's
ABC-TV series *The Julie Andrews Hour* and her 1974 film *The Tamarind Seed*).

S31   *Concert Appearance*. London Palladium. June 9-19, 1976.

S32   *Concert Appearance*. Caesar's Palace, Las Vegas. August 12-18,
1976.

S33   *Galaconcert*. Kongresshaus-Saal, Zurich, Switzerland. December 13,
1976.

S34   *Concert Appearance*. Westchester Premiere Theatre, Tarrytown, New
York. August 24-28, 1977.

S35   *Concert Appearance*. New Greek Theatre, Los Angeles. September
11, 1977.

S36   *Japanese Concert Tour*. Tokyo, Osaka, Sapporo, Fukuoka.
September 19-October 2, 1977.

S37   *Silver Jubilee Royal Variety Gala*. London Palladium. November 21,
1977.

S38   *The Sound of Nysen*. Nysen, Norway. 8/26/78. Benefit concert for
the Nysen Red Cross.

S39   *Lerner and Loewe: A Very Special Evening*. Winter Garden Theatre,
New York. May 14, 1979 (single performance)

Cast: Julie Andrews, D'Jamin Bartlett, Kitty Carlisle, John Cullum, Agnes De Mille,
Janet Eilber, The American Dance Machine, Alfred Drake, Douglas Fairbanks Jr.,
Tovah Feldshuh, Hermoine Gingold, Rex Harrison, Louis Jourdan, George Rose,
Reid Shelton, Alan Jay Lerner.

Songs: From *Camelot* -- "I Wonder What the King is Doing Tonight," "How to Handle a Woman," "I Loved You Once in Silence," "If Ever I Would Leave You," "Camelot," Medley; From *Brigadoon*: -- "Almost Like Being in Love," "The Love of My Life," "The Wedding Dance," "Come to Me... Bend to Me," Medley; From *My Fair Lady*: -- "On the Street Where You Live," "With a Little Bit of Luck," "Show Me," "Wouldn't it Be Loverly," "I Could Have Danced All Night," "I've Grown Accustomed to Her Face"; From *Gigi* -- "Thank Heaven For Little Girls," "I Remember it Well," "The Night They Invented Champagne"; From *Paint Your Wagon*: -- "I Still See Eliza," "They Call the Wind Maria," Medley.

S40   *Because We Care*. Los Angeles. 1/29/80. Julie was among other participants in this benefit concert for Operation California.

S41   *Invitation to the Dance*. New York. November, 1980. Julie appeared with Rudolph Nureyev in this song/ballet performance taped before a live audience for telecasting (see **T46**).

S42   *Japanese Concert Tour*. 2/21/80 through 3/4/80. Festival Hall in Osaka; Niigata; Nippon Budokan Hall and Shinjuku Kosei Nenkin Hall in Tokyo.

S43   *Academy Awards 1983*.   Dorothy Chandler Pavillion. Los Angeles, CA. 4/11/83 (broadcast live over ABC-TV). Julie appeared in the audience as a nominee for Best Actress (*Victor/Victoria*), but didn't win.

S44   *Concert Appearance*. Hartford, Connecticut. 5/23/84. Julie performed with the New American Orchestra.

S45   *Tony Awards*. New York. 6/6/84. Julie appeared with her *Victor/Victoria* costar Robert Preston for this live telecast. She sang "Send in the Clowns."

S46   *One Night Only*. Los Angeles. 6/15/84. Julie and Carol Burnett appeared in this benefit concert for Operation California's fifth anniversary.

S47   *Benefit Performance*. Beverly Hills, CA. 3/3/85. Julie appeared in a benefit for the John Douglas French Foundation for Alzheimer's Disease. Held at the Beverly Hills Hotel.

S48   *Placido Domingo and Friends*. Hollywood, CA. August, 1986 (single performance at the Universal Amphitheatre). This benefit concert was held to raise money for victims of the disastrous 1986 Mexico earthquake. Julie appeared, along with Frank Sinatra, Kirk Douglas, John Denver, Paragon (a Mexican singing group), and Jack Elliott conducting the New American Orchestra. Domingo had lost relatives in the earthquake and had already raised more than $2 million for victims. In its review of the concert, *Variety* (8/20/86) said "The reasons for the concert were laudable; the results, however, were uneven." Domingo and Julie's *West Side Story* medley was termed "dull." Julie was described as "prettily gowned and sang sweetly," but, according to the reviewer, nothing of her personality "made it past the footlights."

S49   *A Captivating Evening With Julie Andrews (Concert Tour)*. After a
five-year absence, Julie returned to the concert stage for this one-woman show. Stops
included the Valley Forge Music Fair in Philadelphia, PA (10/29-11/1/87), Bally's
Grand Opera House in Atlantic City, New Jersey (11/13-15/87), Westbury Music Fair
in Long Island, New York (11/18-21/87), Jackie Gleason Theatre of the Performing
Arts in Miami, FL (1/6-17/88), Chicago Theatre in Chicago, IL (1/28-31/88), and
Northrup Auditorium in Minneapolis, MN (2/10-11/88).
       Many reviewers suggested that the show should play on Broadway, following
in the footsteps of such successful star appearances as Lena Horne, Liza Minnelli,
and Shirley MacLaine. However, the show never was pitched for a Broadway
engagement. The structure of the show was a summary of Julie's career, from
beginning to present, told in song and dialogue, with Julie backed by a 39-piece
orchestra.
       The repertoire included contemporary songs ("Come Rain or Come Shine"),
music hall satire ("Don't Put Your Daughter on the Stage, Miss Worthington") and
the expected standards from *My Fair Lady, Camelot, Thoroughly Modern Millie, The
Sound of Music, Mary Poppins*, et al.
       With few exceptions, the reviews of the concert were highly complementary.
In *Hollywood Reporter* (12/2/87), Morna Murphy-Martell said that Julie is "always a
class act," who "shows great respect for her stardom," which Julie was said to
attribute mostly to "incredible luck." However, Martel found that with her "poise,
genuine rapport with her audience, and uniquely beautiful voice," the luck is "all on
our side."
       In the *Chicago Sun-Times* (1/29/88), Don McLeese called Julie "thoroughly
delightful." He continued that those who expected the concert to be too saccharine
could "rest assured that she has greater gifts to share." He said that he found it "hard
to resist" an artist whose enjoyment of her work is as obvious as Julie's.
       However, Larry Kart of the *Chicago Tribune* (1/24/88), had some
reservations: ("an A-plus performer gives a B-plus performance.") He found Julie's
vocal performance "immaculate," but felt that the dramatic portions of the concert
"kept going in and out of focus." Nonetheless, he found Julie to be "a better, more
personal singer than she used to be -- a performer whose future...lies ahead."

S50   *Museum of Broadcasting: Fifth Annual Television Festival*. Los
Angeles CA. March 9, 1988. Julie appeared on the opening night of this event to
discuss her 1962 CBS-TV special, *Julie and Carol at Carnegie Hall* (see **T11**), which
was screened as the opening program of the festival. The three-week event, designed
to honor distinguished television programs both past and present, was open to the
public, but was sold out almost as soon as it was announced. The festival ran through
March 31.

S51   *American Film Institute Salute to Jack Lemmon*. Beverly Hills, CA.
March 10, 1988 (single performance). Julie served as the hostess for the AFI's
annual salute to an accomplished film artist, which aired as a CBS-TV special in
May, 1988 (see **T54**).

Television Appearances

T01 *Ford Star Jubilee: High Tor* (3/10/56; CBS-TV; 90 minutes)

Bing Crosby, Julie, and Everett Sloane starred in this musical adaptation of Maxwell Anderson's 1937 Broadway play of the same name. Music by Arthur Schwartz. Lyrics by Maxwell Anderson. Orchestrations and Conducting: Joseph J. Lilley. The story involves the ghost of a sixteenth-century Dutch girl who comes to the aid of a man called Van Dorn. The man is trying to fend off a group of people who are trying to buy his mountain, High Tor. See *Discography* (**D05**) for a complete list of musical numbers.

Cast
Van Dorn	Bing Crosby
Lise	Julie Andrews
Judith	Nancy Olson
DeWitt	Everett Sloane
Biggs	Hans Conreid
Skimmerhorn	Lloyd Corigan
Captain	John Picaroll

T02 *The Toast of the Town* (11/11/56; CBS-TV; 60 minutes)

Julie guested on this early Ed Sullivan variety show. From *My Fair Lady*, she sang "Without You" and "I Could Have Danced All Night." She appeared on *The Ed Sullivan Show* in 1961 to perform songs from *Camelot*. (See **T08** in this section.)

T03 *Rodgers and Hammerstein's Cinderella* (3/31/57 CBS-TV; 90 minutes)

This was the premiere showing of the only musical created by Richard Rodgers (music) and Oscar Hammerstein II (lyrics) especially for television. Directed by Ralph Nelson. Remade in 1965 by CBS starring Lesley Ann Warren as Cinderella, and an all-new cast. Alice Ghostley, who played one of the evil stepsisters, reteamed with Julie as a regular on the 1972-73 ABC-TV variety series,

The Julie Andrews Hour. (See **T28** in this section.) See *Discography* (**D05**) for a complete list of musical numbers.

Cast:

Cinderella	Julie Andrews
Prince	Jon Cypher
Fairy Godmother	Edith Adams
Stepmother	Ilka Chase
Stepsisters	Kaye Ballard
	Alice Ghostley
Queen	Dorothy Stickney
King	Howard Lindsay

T04   *Crescendo* **(1957; CBS-TV; 90 minutes)**

This 90-minute special starred Rex Harrison, Julie, and Stanley Holloway. Harrison was a man from England visiting the U.S. and being exposed to a wide range of American music styles. Julie and Holloway performed a medley from *My Fair Lady.*

T05   *The Jack Benny Hour* **(5/23/59; CBS-TV ; 60 minutes)**

Julie guested along with Phil Silvers on this Jack Benny hour special, featuring music, song, and comedy. Julie sang "I'm Just Wild About Harry" and "A'int We Got Fun." Producer/Director: Bud Yorkin. Music director: David Rose. Writers: David Rose, George Balzer, Hal Goodman, Al Gordon.

T06   *The Gentle Flame (12/59);* **BBC in England; 60 minutes)**

Julie appeared as the match girl Trissa in Francis Essex's musical adaptation of a fairy tale by Hans Christian Anderson.

T07   *The Fabulous 50's* **(1/31/60; CBS-TV; 2 hours)**

Variety special saluting the decade of the 50s. Appearing with Julie were: Shelly Berman, Betty Comden, Henry Fonda, Jackie Gleason, Rex Harrison, Elaine May, Mike Nichols, Suzy Parker, and Eric Sevareid. Producer: Leland Hayward. Associate Producer: Marshall Jamison. Director: Norman Jewison. Music Directors: Alfredo Anotonini, Franz Allers (*My Fair Lady, Camelot*), John Lesko, and Jay Blackton. Writers: Max Wolk, A. J. Russell, Stephen Sondheim.

T08   *The Ed Sullivan Show* **(3/61; CBS-TV; 60 minutes)**

Making her second CBS appearance as a guest of Ed Sullivan (see **T02** in this section), Julie appeared, along with Richard Burton to perform the "What Do the Simple Folk Do?" number from *Camelot.* Up to that point, *Camelot* had not done spectacular business on Broadway, where it had opened in December, 1960. Immediately after this Sullivan show aired, lines began forming at the boxoffice the very next day, and the show became a hit.

T09 *The Garry Moore Show* **(Spring/61; CBS-TV; 60 minutes**

Julie first cavorted with Carol Burnett on television in this popular weekly variety series, singing "Big D" from the Frank Loesser musical *Most Happy Fella*. The number was repeated in Julie and Carol's Carnegie Hall special (see **T11**). Julie's appearance on Moore's show was so well received that he signed her up for five more episodes the following season.

T10 *The Broadway of Lerner and Loewe*
(2/62; BBC in England; 60 minutes)

Julie appeared in this British musical special honoring the composers of *My Fair Lady* and *Camelot*, the first of many such salutes she would participate in both onstage and on television in the coming years.

T11 *Julie and Carol at Carnegie Hall* **(6/11/62; CBS-TV; 60 minutes)**

Julie costarred with Carol Burnett, another popular Broadway/television performer, in this hour-long special of comedy and songs, taped before a live audience at New York's Carnegie Hall. The program won Emmy Awards (see *Awards and Nominations*) and the Rose D'Or from the Montreaux International Television Festival.

In the New York *Times* (6/12/62), Jack Gould said: "a program of infectious lilt...inevitably revived memories of TV's melodic union of Mary Martin and Ethel Merman." Julie was called "nothing less than captivating in her delicate and enchanting rendition of 'So Long at the Fair.'" The highlight was said to be the "priceless" medley of musical comedy numbers."

Julie and Carol reunited for a 1971 CBS variety special (see listing **T24** in this section), and as this book goes to press, a third Burnett/ Andrews special is in discussion. (*Note*: The Carnegie Hall special was screened on March 9, 1988 in Los Angeles as the kickoff performance of the Museum of Broadcasting's Fifth Annual Television festival. See *Stage Appearances* **[S51]** for more details.)

Executive Producer: Bob Banner. Producer: Joe Hamilton. Music Director: Irwin Kostal (who scored the *Mary Poppins* and *Sound of Music* films and Julie's 1965 NBC-TV special with Gene Kelly). Writers: Mike Nichols, Ken Welch. Choreographer: Ernest Flatt.

See *Discography* **(D14)** for a complete list of musical numbers.

T12 *Academy Awards 1964* **(4/13/64; ABC-TV; three hours)**

The show was broadcast live from the Santa Monica Civic Auditorium in California. Appearing at the Academy Awards for the first time, Julie presented the Best Foreign Film award to Federico Fellini for *8 1/2*. She did not make her film debut until September of that year (*Mary Poppins*). However, she would become a familiar face at the Oscar ceremonies over the next few years.

T13 *The Andy Williams Show* **(11/30/64; NBC-TV; 60 minutes)**

Julie guested on this variety series, receiving an Emmy nomination for "Individual Achievement in Entertainment -- Actors and Performers," but no award.

T14 *The Julie Andrews Show* **(11/28/65; NBC-TV; 60 minutes)**

Variety special guest starring Gene Kelly and the New Christy Minstrels. Producer/Director: Alan Handley. Musical Director: Irwin Kostal (*Mary Poppins,*

Sound of Music, Julie and Carol at Carnegie Hall). Writers: Bill Persky and Sam Denoff (*The Dick Van Dyke Show*). Won two Emmy awards and several nominations. (See *Awards and Nominations* chapter.)

T15   *Academy Awards 1965* **(4/5/65; ABC-TV; 3 hours, plus)**

For the first time, Julie was very much in the Oscar spotlight. This was not so much for her own Best Actress nomination (for *Mary Poppins*), but more so for a double controversy: her not being cast for the film of *My Fair Lady*, and the Academy nomination shutout of Audrey Hepburn (who got Julie's *Lady* role). Referring to Jack L. Warner, who cast *Lady*, a Warner Bros. film, emcee Bob Hope quipped, "Julie Andrews is up for *Mary Poppins*, or How I Learned to Stop Worrying and Love Jack Warner."

Good sport Audrey Hepburn appeared to present the Best Actor award to Rex Harrison for *My Fair Lady*. Julie attended the ceremonies with her then-husband Tony Walton, who lost out in the Costume Design category for *Mary Poppins* to *My Fair Lady's* Cecil Beaton.

The song sung by Julie and Dick Van Dyke in *Poppins* ("Chim Chim Cheree") was performed at the ceremonies by the New Christie Minstrels, and eventually picked up the Best Song award for composers Richard M. Sherman and Robert B. Sherman. Despite the fact that it was a highly competitive Oscar year with several excellent films contending (*Zorba the Greek, Becket, Dr. Strangelove*), it was very much a *Fair Lady/Poppins* evening, with Julie, Harrison, and Hepburn so prominently in the spotlight and with the tally of major awards (8 to *Lady*, 5 to *Poppins*) leaving few awards left for other films.

Despite some critics' predictions that Kim Stanley (*Seance on a Wet Afternoon*) or Debbie Reynolds (*The Unsinkable Molly Brown*) might upset Julie's expected victory, Sidney Poitier offered no surprise when he opened the Best Actress envelope to announce Julie as the winner. Julie's acceptance speech opened with the following statement: "I know you Americans are famous for your hospitality, but this is really ridiculous...I only know where to start...Mr. Disney gets the biggest thank you..." and concluded with thanks to everyone "for making me feel truly welcome in this country." (She must have had second thoughts about that statement a few years later when the media went after her with a vengeance, following the failures of *Star!* and *Darling Lili*.)

The show was telecast live from the Santa Monica Civic Auditorium in California.

T16   *Academy Awards 1966* **(4/18/66; ABC-TV; 3 hours, plus)**

For the second year in a row, Julie was very much the belle of the ball at the Oscars, due to the spectacular success of *The Sound of Music* and her neck-to-neck battle with another English Julie (Christie, for *Darling*) for Best Actress honors. Many critics felt that Julie's performance in *Music* was stronger than that of *Poppins*, but winning two back-to-back awards is an Oscar rarity. (Luise Rainer managed the feat, as did Katharine Hepburn.) Still, it was one of the tightest Oscar races ever, providing edge-of-your-seat suspense.

Julie attended the ceremony with *Sound of Music* producer Saul Chaplin, and went up to the podium twice before the Best Actress category was announced. She accepted the Best Director award from Shirley MacLaine for *Sound of Music's* Robert Wise, who was busily at work on *The Sand Pebbles*, and unable to attend. Moments later, she appeared to present the Best Actor award to Lee Marvin for *Cat Ballou*. Then she nervously waited backstage for the Best Actress announcement by Rex Harrison, as there wasn't time to return to her seat. Harrison opened the envelope to announce that the winner was Julie...Christie.

Julie's disappointment was probably abated a bit a few minutes later when Jack Lemmon announced that the Best Picture was *The Sound of Music*, and Saul Chaplin accepted the award. Second Oscar or not, Julie was still at the top of the Hollywood heap.

The show was telecast live from the Santa Monica Civic Auditorium in California.

T17   *Academy Awards 1968* (4/10/68; ABC-TV; 3 hours, plus)

Though still very much a superstar, Julie was not the center of attention at the 1968 awards. The trend in Hollywood films was already shifting from musicals to hard-edged realism and violence in provocative adult fare. Among major contendors that year were *Bonnie and Clyde, In the Heat of the Night, The Graduate,* and *In Cold Blood.*

Julie's *Thoroughly Modern Millie* won several nominations, but the only major one was for Supporting Actress (Carol Channing). Rex Harrison's *Doctor Doolittle* musical miraculously managed a Best Picture nomination, but no one took it seriously, as the picture had not been well received by either critics or audiences. The Warners film of *Camelot* (with Vanessa Redgrave in Julie's stage role) had several technical nominations. Both *Millie* and *Camelot* managed to win a handful of technical awards, while *Doctor Doolittle* had to settle for Best Song (Leslie Bricusse's "Talk to the Animals.")

Angela Lansbury, a hot musical star at the time, thanks to Broadway's *Mame*, appeared with the Ronald Field dancers to perform Julie's title song from *Thoroughly Modern Millie.*

Julie's duty as presenter was the Best Picture award, which went to producer Walter Mirisch (who Julie had worked with on *Hawaii*) for *In the Heat of the Night.*

An important message began to appear at the Oscars, which would dramatically affect the course of Julie's career: Musicals were out and message pictures were in. (The following year, *Oliver!* won Best Picture, but was the last musical to date to accomplish that feat.)

The show was telecast live from the Santa Monica Civic Auditorium in California.

T18   *The Julie Andrews Special* (11/9/69; NBC-TV; 60 minutes)

Also known as *An Evening With Julie Andrews and Harry Belafonte.* Variety special co-starring Harry Belafonte. Producer/Director: Gower Champion. Musical Director: Michel Legrand. Writer: Robert Emmett.

T19   *Tony Awards* (6/6/70; CBS-TV; 90 minutes)

Julie appeared as co-hostess for this live telecast from New York.

T20   *The David Frost Show* (7/6/70; ABC-TV; 90 minutes)

Julie and future husband Blake Edwards were interviewed on this talk show, shortly after the opening of their first film collaboration, *Darling Lili.*

T21   *A World of Love* (12/22/70; CBS-TV; 60 minutes)

Christmas variety show saluting children all over the world. Co-hosts: Shirley MacLaine and Bill Cosby. Julie guested, along with Richard Burton, Barbra

Streisand, Harry Belafonte, Audrey Hepburn, and Florence Henderson. Producer:
Alexander H. Cohen. Director: Clark Jones. Music Director: Elliot Lawrence.
Writer: Hildy Parks.

T22   *Disney World: A Gala Opening -- Disneyland East;*
                 10/29/71; NBC-TV; 90 minutes

  Variety special marking the opening of Disney World in Florida. Julie
guested along with Bob Hope, Glen Campbell, Buddy Hackett, and Jonathan Winters.
Producer/Director: Robert Scheerer. Music Director: Dave Grusin.

T23   *The David Frost Show* **(11/18/71; ABC-TV; 90 minutes)**

  Julie is interviewed by Frost, along with James Coburn and Sally Struthers.

T24   *Julie and Carol at Lincoln Center* **(12/7/71; CBS-TV; 60 minutes)**

  Variety Special reuniting Julie and Carol Burnett. Taped before a live
audience at Lincoln Center's Philharmonic Hall on July 1, 1971. Producer: Joe
Hamilton. Director: Dave Powers. Music Director: Peter Matz. Original musical
material by Ken and Mitzi Welch. Writers: Bob Ellison, Marty Farrell.
Choreographer: Ernest Flatt. Julie and Carol first appeared together in a 1962 CBS
variety special (see listing **T11** in this section), and as this book goes to press, a third
CBS Burnett/ Andrews special is in discussion. See the *Awards and Nominations*
section for a list of Emmy awards and nominations. See *Discography* **(D26)** for a
complete list of musical numbers.

T25   *The Dick Cavett Show* **(12/18/71; ABC-TV; 90 minutes)**

  Julie and husband Blake Edwards appeared on this late night talk show.

T26   *Emmy Awards* **(5/14/72; NBC-TV; two hours)**

  Julie appeared to accept an acting award for Glenda Jackson.

T27   *Julie!* **(8/24/72; ABC-TV;); 60 minutes**

  Documentary special about Julie, obviously intended as a plug for her about-
to-debut weekly variety series on ABC-TV. Producer/Director: Blake Edwards.
Music Director: Nelson Riddle. Choreography: Tony Charmoli.

T28   **The Julie Andrews Hour**
                 (9/13/72 to 4/28/73; ABC-TV; 60 minutes weekly)

  Julie enthusiastically launched this weekly variety series as part of a deal with
producer Sir Lew Grade's ITC Productions, which was originally to include the series
plus one film per year. (Only *The Tamarind Seed* in 1974 came to fruition.) The
series won almost unanimous critical praise and several Emmy Awards, but never
attracted a large enough audience to last more than one season (24 episodes). ABC
shifted it from Wednesday night to Saturday in midseason to no avail. (See the
Awards and Nominations section for a complete list of Emmy wins and nominations.)

In *TV Guide* (10/26/72), Cleveland Amory wrote, "Whether you're a fan of Julie Andrews or not...you have to admit...she has class...The show has brought back something which has lately been in short supply...style."

Producers: Nick Vanoff, William O. Harbach. Director: Bill Davis. Announcer: Dick Tufeld. Music Director: Nelson Riddle. Special Music Material: Dick Williams. Music Associate: Ian Frasier. Choreography: Tony Charmoli. Writers: John Aylesworth, Jay Burton, George Bloom, Bob Ellison, Hal Goodman, Larry Klein, and Lile Garrett. Art Direction: Jim Timokins. Regulars: Alice Ghostley (who appeared as one of the evil stepsisters in Julie's 1957 CBS-TV musical special, *Rodger's and Hammerstein's Cinderella*), Rich Little, the Tony Charmoli Dancers, the Dick Williams Singers.

Following is an episode-by-episode summary of all broadcasts of the series.

The Julie Andrews Hour -- Episode-by-Episode

- 9/13/72

  The premiere show was an Emmy-award winning one-woman showcase for Julie, who performed scenes and songs from her various stage and film roles (including *My Fair Lady, Mary Poppins, Star!, The Sound of Music*, and *Camelot*.) Among other sings, Julie performed "Wouldn't It Be Loverly?", "Do Re Mi," "Burlington Bertie from Bow," "If Ever I Would Leave You," and a *Boy Friend* medley.

- 9/20/72

  Guests: Carl Reiner, Mama Cass Elliott. Sketches: a spoof of the film *All About Eve*, a recitation of movie cliches, and a salute to those born under the sign of Aquarius. Songs: "And This is My Beloved," "You're Going to Hear From Me" (Julie), a medley with Mama Cass, and "It's Today" (Ensemble).

- 9/27/72

  Guests: Jack Cassidy, Ken Berry. Theme: Salute to the past of Broadway and Hollywood. Sketches: Ken and Julie spoof Astaire and Rogers; Jack as Flo Ziegfield escorting Julie to Delmonico's; Rich Little mimes Bogart. Songs: "I Have Dreamed" and Scottich medley (Julie), "Lullaby of Broadway," "I Know Darn Well I Can Do Without You" (Julie, Jack), Love song medley (Ensemble).

- 10/4/72

  Guest: Don Rickles, who joined Julie in a Noel Coward spoof called "Not So Private Lives.

- 10/11/72

  Guest: Robert Goulet (his first appearance with Julie since Broadway's *Camelot*). Theme: Salute to composers Irving Berlin, Cole Porter, Richard Rodgers, and Jerome Kern. Songs: "Alexander's Ragtime Band," "Shall We Dance?" (Julie), "There's No Business Like Show Business," "Too Darn Hot," "Night and Day," "Where or When," "Fascinating Rhythm," *Porgy and Bess* medley (Julie, Robert).

- 10/18/72

  Guest: Steve Lawrence. Skit: Steve as a brash Yank flier and Julie as a music hall girl in a *Darling Lili*-styled spy caper. Salutes to several celebrities, including Laurel and Hardy, Jeannette MacDonald and Nelson Eddy, and the Marx Brothers. Songs: Until it's Time For You to Go," "Men Like You" (Julie), "Applause," "We'll Meet Again," Oscar medley (Julie, Steve).

- 10/25/72

  Guests: Diahann Carroll, Phyllis Diller. Theme: Salute to women songwriters and band singers. Songs: "Two Ladies in De Shade of Da Banana Tree" (Julie,Diahann), Burt Bacharach medley (Julie, Diahann, Phyllis), football medley (Ensemble).

The Julie Andrews Hour -- Episode-by-Episode (continued)

- 11/1/72
  Guests: Dan Dailey, Mama Cass Elliott. Skits: a spoof of Dan's movies; Dan and Julie as struggling vaudevillians; Julie and Alice Ghostley as incompatible roommates. Songs: "This Nearly Was Mine" (Julie), "Alone Again" (Mama Cass), Simon and Garfunkel medley (Julie, Mama Cass), "You Were Meant For Me," "Keep Your Sunny Side Up" (Julie, Dan), "Bill Bailey" (Ensemble).

- 11/8/72
  Guests: Robert Goulet, Joel Grey. A musical salute to Lerner and Loewe includes songs from *Gigi, Paint Your Wagon, Camelot, Brigadoon,* and *My Fair Lady.* Joel appears as George M. Cohan and Robert as a Canadian Mountie in separate sketches. The ensemble performs a medley from *Cabaret.*

- 11/22/72
  Guests: Donald O'Connor, the Young Americans, and Adriana Caselotti (the original voice of Disney's *Snow White*). Theme: Salute to Walt Disney. Songs: "He's a Tramp" (Julie), "I've Got No Strings," *Mary Poppins* medley (Julie, Donald), "I'm Wishing," "Someday My Prince Will Come," (Julie, Adriana), Medley (Young Americans), "When You Wish Upon a Star," "Zip a Dee Doo Da" (Ensemble).

- 11/29/72
  Guests: Harry Belafonte, guitarist Sivuca. Sketches: Harry and Julie as two lonely people; Julie mimes Beatrice Lillie. Songs: "Fever," "Yesterday" (Julie), "Blowin' in the Wind" (Harry), "Suzanne," "Mr. Bojangles" (Harry, Sivuca).

- 12/6/72
  Guests: Tom and Dick Smothers, Jack Cassidy. Sketches: a Roaring 20s salute; a cocktail lounge. Songs: "Ain't We Got Fun" (Julie, Jack), "Making Whoopee" (Julie, Dick), "Charleston" (Julie, Dancers), "Talk to the Animals," Gilbert and Sullivan medley (Ensemble).

- 12/13/72
  Guests: Tony Randall, Keith Michell. Salutes to Noel Coward, English music halls, and Broadway musicals. Songs: "Waitin' at the Church," "Twentieth Century Blues" (Julie), "How Are Things in Glocca Mora?" "Poor Little Rich Girl" (Tony), "The Impossible Dream," "Nina" (Keith), "Wunderbar" (Julie, Tony), "Tradition" (Dancers)

- 12/20/72
  Guest: James Stewart. Cameos: Joel Grey, Carl Reiner, Mama Cass Elliott, Jack Cassidy. Christmas show (repackaged several years later as a syndicated special -- see listing **T45**). Examining ways of celebrating Christmas in the England of Charles Dickens and in modern day small towns. Songs: "Jingle Bells" and Christmas medley (Julie),

The Julie Andrews Hour -- Episode-by-Episode (continued)

"The Christmas Song" (Julie, Jimmy), "It Came Upon the Midnight Clear" (Mama Cass), "I Heard the Bells on Christmas Day" (Carl), "Caroling Caroling" (Jack), The Stingiest Man in Town" (Alice Ghostley).

● 12/27/72   Repeat from 10/11/72.

● 1/10/73   Guest: Keith Michell, who joins Julie in classic scenes from drama and literature. These include Shakespeare's *The Taming of the Shrew*, Noel Coward's *Cavalcade*, Oscar Wilde's *The Importance of Being Earnest*, and A. A. Milne's *The King's Breakfast*. Songs: "On a Clear Day" (Julie), "What Will You Leave?" (Keith), "Two on the Aisle," "Dancing in the Dark," "Dancing on the Ceiling," "Mack the Knife" (Julie, Keith).

● 1/20/73   Guests: Jim Nabors, Eydie Gorme, Maria von Trapp (who Julie portrayed in *The Sound of Music*). The opening scenes from *The Sound of Music* are shown. A skit spoofs *Gone With the Wind*. Songs: "Do Re Mi," "The Sound of Music," "Whistle a Happy Tune" (Julie) "Why Was I Born?" (Eydie), "Edelweiss" (Julie, Maria), "Make Believe" (Jim), "I Am Woman," Rain medley (Julie, Eydie).

● 1/27/73   Guests: Peggy Lee, Robert Goulet. Salutes to Broadway producer David Merrick and to Sagittarians. "I'm Gonna Wash That Man Right Out of My Hair," "Summertime," "Let Me Entertain You," "Love Makes the World Go Round" (Julie), "Someone Who Cares," "Who Will Buy?" (Peggy), "Fanny" (Robert), "The Candy Man," "Before the Parade Passes By" (Julie, Peggy, Robert), "Take Me Along," "Together" (Ensemble).

● 2/3/73   Guests: Sid Caesar, John Davidson. Sketches: a *Godfather* spoof; Sid in his German professor character. Songs: "On the Sunny Side of the Street," "Baubles Bangles and Beads," "Get Happy" (Julie).

● 2/10/73   Guests: Angela Lansbury, Steve Lawrence, Brazilian composer-guitarist Luiz Bonfa. Julie and Angela salute great ladies of show business: Mae West, Sophie Tucker, Ethel Merman, Judy Garland, Carmen Miranda, Eleanor Powell, Helen Morgan, and the Dolly Sisters. Songs: "All the Things You Are" (Julie), "I Don't Want to Know" (Angela), "I Got Rhythm" (Julie, Angela), "Watch What Happens" (Julie, Steve, Luiz), "Batacuda" (Luiz), "To Be a Performer" (Ensemble).

The Julie Andrews Hour -- Episode-by-Episode (continued)

● 2/17/73

Guests: Sandy Duncan, Sergio Franchi, and Muppetts Thog and Rowlf. Salute to composer Jerome Kern. Songs: "Smoke Gets in Your Eyes," "The Last Time I Saw Paris" (Julie), "I'm Old Fashioned" (Sandy), "Old Man River" (Sergio), "The Last Blues Song," "Life Upon the Wicked Stage" (Julie, Sandy), "The Song Is You" (Julie, Sergio), "Look for the Silver Lining" (Ensemble).

● 2/24/73

Repeat of premiere episode (from 9/13/72).

● 3/3/73

Guest: Sammy Davis Jr. Songs: "It's a Musical World," "Just You Wait," "How Are Things in Glocca Morra?" (Julie), "If I Were a Rich Man," "A Hymn to Him," "When I'm Not Near the Girl I Love" (Sammy), "Sue Me," "Trouble," "Tea For Two," "Be a Clown," "A Couple of Swells," medleys of spring songs and Blood, Sweat, and Tears tunes (Julie, Sammy).

● 3/17/73

Guests: Carol Lawrence, Steve Lawrence. Salute to the 30s, including candid film clips of W. C. Fields, John Wayne, Kate Smith, and Lawrence Welk. Songs: "Lambeth Walk" (Julie), "Ten Cents a Dance," "Stompin' at the Savoy" (Carol), "Eadie was a Lady" (Steve), "Dipsy Doodle" (Julie, Carol), "Embraceable You," "You're Driving Me Crazy" (Julie, Steve).

● 3/24/73

Guests: Donald O'Connor, Harve Presnell. Salute to composer Frank Loesser. Songs: "Something's Gotta Give," "But Not For Me," "Somebody Somewhere" (Julie), "Once in Love with Amy" (Donald), "When I Look in Your Eyes," "Luck Be a Lady" (Harve), Street medley (Julie, Donald), "Out of My Dreams," "My Heart is So Full of You" (Julie, Harve), "I Believe in You," "The Brotherhood of Man" (Julie, Harve, Donald).

● 3/31/73

Guest: Henry Mancini. One segment includes bloopers taped during the season. "Whistling Away the Dark," *Peter Gunn* and *Pink Panther* themes (Julie), "The Days of Wine and Roses," "Sometime," "Once Upon a Time," "Charade," "The Sweetheart Tree," "Two For the Road," "Nothing to Lose," "Dear Heart," "Moon River" (Julie, Henry).

● 4/7/73

Repeat from 9/27/72.

● 4/14/73

Repeat from 1/20/73.

● 4/21/73

Repeat from 11/22/72.

● 4/28/73

Repeat from 2/17/73.

T29   *Academy Awards 1973* (April, 1973; ABC-TV; 3 hours, plus)

After her Hollywood heyday in the mid-60s, this was Julie's first Oscar appearance in several years. Julie and George Stevens announced the Best Director winner (Bob Fossee for *Cabaret*). *Cabaret*, starring Liza Minnelli, briefly brought the musical back to the Oscar forefront. It picked up eight Oscars, but lost the big one (Best Picture) to The *Godfather*. No film musical since then has had major Oscar attention or received a Best Picture nomination. Telecast live from the Dorothy Chandler Pavilion in Los Angeles.

T30   *Julie on Sesame Street* (11/23/73; ABC-TV; 60 minutes)

Variety special. Guest stars included Perry Como, the Muppets, and the Paddy Stone Dancers. Julie did a Broadway medley with the Muppets and Como sang his hit of the day, "And I Love You So." Executive Producer: Blake Edwards. Producers: Gary Smith and Dwight Hemion. Director: Dwight Hemion. Music Director: Jack Parnell. Writers: Jon Stone, Marty Farrell, Bob Ellison.

T31   *Julie's Christmas Special* (12/73; ABC-TV; 60 minutes)

Variety special. Guest stars included Peggy Lee and Peter Ustinov.

T32   *Oscar Winners* (3/74; CBS-TV; 60 minutes)

Julie and director Robert Wise appeared to talk about *The Sound of Music*.

T33   *Julie and Dick in Covent Garden* (4/21/74; ABC-TV; 60 minutes)

Variety special co-starring Dick Van Dyke (his first appearance with Julie since *Mary Poppins* in 1964). Guest: Carl Reiner. Executive Producer/Director: Blake Edwards. Producers: Dennis Vance and Bill Glaze. Music: Jack Parnell. Writers: Marty Farrell, Frank Waldman, Dick Hills. Art Director: Peter Roden. Choreographer: Paddy Stone.

T34   *The Today Show* (6/4/74; NBC-TV; two hours)

Barbara Walters interviewed Julie on this daytime morning show.

T35   *Julie and Jackie -- How Sweet It Is* (1974; ABC-TV; 60 minutes)

Variety special co-starring Jackie Gleason. Producer: Gary Smith. Director: Dwight Hemion.

T36   *Julie -- My Favorite Things* (4/18/75; ABC-TV; 60 minutes)

Variety special. Guest stars included Peter Sellers and the Muppets. Sellers played Inspector Clouseau in Blake Edwards' popular *Pink Panther* series, which Julie *almost* appeared in --twice. (See Appendix B.) Sellers also was to be Julie's costar in *Victor/Victoria*, but he died before filming started in 1981, and the part went to Robert Preston. Producer: Bob Wells. Director: Blake Edwards. Music Director:

Ian Fraser. Music Conductor: Jack Parnell. Writers: Frank Waldman, Bob Wells, Blake Edwards.

T37   *The Merv Griffin Show* **(11/75; syndicated; 90 minutes)**

Merv Griffin interviewed Julie during this tribute to director Robert Wise (*The Sound of Music*).

T38   *Oscar's Best Movies* **(2/13/77; ABC-TV; 30 minutes)**

Retrospective of Oscar-winning films. Julie introduced the segment on musicals and comedies.

T39   *Royal Variety Show* **(11/77; BBC in England)**

Julie appeared in this British special from the London Palladium.

T40   *Julie Andrews: One Step into Spring* **(3/9/78; CBS-TV; 60 minutes**

Variety special. Guest stars included Alan King, Leslie Uggams, and Leo Sayer. Executive Producer: Bob Banner. Producer: Steve Pouliot. Director: Jeff Margolis. Choreographer: Paddy Stone.

T41   *The Sound of Nysen* **(8/26/78; Norwegian TV; Nysen, Norway)**

Julie performed in this benefit concert for the Red Cross, telecast live in Norway.

T42   *The Muppet Show* **(1978; Syndicated; 30 minutes)**

The Muppets returned the favor of appearing on two of Julie's previous specials by having her as a guest on theirs.

T43   *Good Morning America* **(10/10/79; ABC-TV; two hours)**

Pat Collins interviewed Julie on this weekday early morning show.

T44   *The Dinah Shore Show* **(10/23/79; NBC-TV; 30 minutes)**

Julie guested on Dinah Shore's daytime talk show.

T45   *Merry Christmas...With Love, Julie* **(12/79; Syndicated; 60 minutes)**

A rerun from the 1972/73 *Julie Andrews Hour* series on ABC-TV (see **T28** in this section). Guest stars include Jimmy Stewart, Joel Grey and two *Julie Andrews Hour* regulars: Alice Ghostley and Rich Little.

T46   *The CBS Festival of the Lively Arts For Young People: Julie*
                Andrews' Invitation to the Dance with Rudolf Nuryev (2/30/80;
                CBS-TV; 60 minutes)

Daytime variety special. Guest stars included Rudolph Nuryev, Ann
Reinking, and the Green Grass Cloggers. Directed by Tony Charmoli. Written by
Buzz Kohan. Emmy award winner for Children's Programming. (See *Awards*
section.)

T47   *Bob Hope's Pink Panther Thanksgiving Gala*
                (11/21/82; NBC-TV; 2 hours)

Variety special celebrating the 20th anniversary of Blake Edwards' *Pink
Panther* films. Comedy skits and film clips were spotlighted. Julie guested, along
with Bernadette Peters, Dean Martin, Robert Wagner, Robert Preston, Dudley Moore,
and Willie Nelson. Executive Producer: Bob Hope. Producer: William O'Harbach,
Director: Tony Charmoli. Announcer: John Harlan. Music: Les Brown. Writers:
Gig Henry, Robert L. Mills, Fred S. Fox, Seaman Jacobs.

T48   *Academy Awards 1983* (4/11/83; ABC-TV; three hours)

Broadcast live from the Dorothy Chandler Pavillion in Los Angeles, CA, Julie
appeared in the audience as a nominee for Best Actress (*Victor/Victoria*), but didn't
win.

T49   *Tony Awards* (6/6/84; NBC-TV; two hours)

Julie appeared with her *Victor/Victoria* costar Robert Preston for this live
telecast from New York. She sang "Send in the Clowns."

T50   *A Salute to Henry Mancini* (1987; PBS-TV; 60 minutes)

Julie guested on this special saluting the man who composed the scores from
several of her films, including *Darling Lili, Victor/Victoria, S.O.B.* and *10*.

T51   *Julie Andrews: The Sound of Christmas*
                (12/16/87; ABC-TV; 60 minutes)

This was Julie's first major network special in several years, and it won five
Emmy Awards. To highlight the occasion, much of the special was filmed on
location in the Austrian Alps, locale for *The Sound of Music*. Guest stars included
Placido Domingo, John Denver, and the King's Sisters.
        The reviews were generally excellent. In *TV Guide* (12/11/87), Paul Droesch
said "This hour looks marvelous and doesn't sound bad either, thanks to Andrews and
guests." In *Hollywood Reporter* (12/16/87), Miles Beller called the show: "a seasonal
affair that's pleasant enough as these things go, and not without a charm or three...the
sort of holiday dish that's good ingesting on a seasonal basis." *Variety* (12/18/87)
said that the special reinforced television as an ideal medium for Julie's talent. The
show was called "a combined picture postcard - music video" taking full advantage of
"the fairy-tale province of Salzburg." Julie was said to " revert back to the pristine
veneer of the 60s," which the reviewer felt was appropriate within the context of the
show. He found this shift "infinitely more appealing after her naughty escapades in

hubby Blake Edwards' films." The reviewer quibbled with the use of videotape, which he said gave the picture a "superficial quality."

Julie sang a new song ,"The Sound of Christmas" with the Alps as background, evoking memories of *The Sound of Music*. Two other sequences occurred at the Church of Mondesee where Maria (Julie) was married in the film. Domingo sang "O Holy Night." Julie dueted with the King's Sisters in a parody of "The Twelve Days of Christmas." Julie sang "Edelweiss" with Denver and "Something New in My Life" with Domingo.

Producer: Nick Vanoff. Associate Producers: Rene Lagler and Martin Baker. Director: Dwight Hemion. Music Director: Ian Fraser. Editors: Andy Zall, Mark West, and Bob Jenkis.

T52   *Lerner and Loewe: Broadway's Last Romantics*
           (March, 1988; PBS-TV; 70 minutes)

This documentary special on Broadway lyricist Alan Jay Lerner (1918-1986) and composer Frederick Loewe (1901-1988) followed the career of the famous duo. Focus is on the team's major stage musicals (*Brigadoon, Paint Your Wagon, My Fair Lady, and Camelot*) and film musicals (adaptations of the four previously mentioned stage shows plus *Gigi* and *The Little Prince*, created especially for the screen).

Julie was interviewed regarding *My Fair Lady* and *Camelot*, offering some fascinating behind-the-scenes details about the development of the shows. Audrey Hepburn (*My Fair Lady*) was also interviewed. Both she and Julie commented on the controversy that occurred when Hollywood bypassed Julie for the film version of *Lady* and gave it to Audrey. Julie confided that as much as she wanted the film role, she never really expected to get it.

Clips from the famous 1965 Oscar telecast were shown, with Audrey (who failed to get a Best Actress nomination) presenting the Best Actor Award to Rex Harrison for *My Fair Lady*, and Julie accepting her Best Actress award for *Mary Poppins*. (See listing **T15** in this section for more details.)

Rehearsal and performance clips from *Lady* and *Camelot* added to the interest of the show. Julie was shown being prompted by her vocal coach to get angry at Professor Higgins when singing "Just You Wait." Harrison is depicted throwing a temper tantrum because he is having difficulty singing over the orchestra in his first musical.

TV Guide (3/12/88) called the show "an enjoyable retrospective on their [Lerner and Loewe's] often stormy partnership." Host: Richard Kiley (*The Little Prince*).

T53   *The Second Annual American Comedy Awards*
           (5/17/88; ABC-TV; 2 hours)

Sixteen categories of comedy performers were honored in this special awards program, mounted under difficult conditions due to the 1988 Writer's Guild strike. A segment included a special tribute to Julie's colleague and husband, Producer/Director/Writer Blake Edwards, who received a Lifetime Achievement Award. Anticipating an enjoyable outing based on the previous year's editon of this show, *TV Guide* (5/14/88) said "expect a stageful of celebrities, a certain amount of flash and plenty of professionalism...better than your average awards show."

T54   *The AFI Life Achievement Award: A Salute to Jack Lemmon*;
(5/30/88; CBS-TV; 60 minutes)

Julie served as hostess for this tribute to her *That's Life!* costar, presented
every Spring by the American Film Institute to a distinguished film actor, director, or
producer. The show was videotaped in March in a ceremony at the Beverly Hilton
Hotel in Beverly Hills, then edited down for an hour time slot. Shirley MacLaine,
Michael Douglas, Walter Matthau, Steve Martin, and Chris Lemmon (Jack's son)
appeared to join in the accolades.

TV Guide (5/28/88) said of the show: "(it) has only one thing wrong with it:
it's only an hour long. That isn't nearly enough time to do justice to Lemmon's
extraordinary career." Miles Beller in *Hollywood Reporter* (5/31/88) called the show
"a great rousing roar of a celebration." *Variety* (5/31/88) called it a "snappy
program." Producer: George Stevens Jr. Co-Producer: Jeffrey Lane. Associate
Producer: Michael B. Seligman. Director: Louis J. Horovitz. Writers: George
Stevens Jr. and Jeffrey Lane. Musical Director: Nick Preito. Art Director: Ray
Klausen. Editors: Michael L. Weitzman and Chuck Meyers.

T55   *Gleason: The Great One* (9/17/88; CBS-TV; two hours)

Special saluting Jackie Gleason included clips from many of his past TV
appearances, including the 1974 ABC-TV special that he starred in with Julie (*Julie
and Jackie -- How Sweet It Is*; see **T35**).

Discography

Following is a chronological list of the albums recorded by Julie Andrews (and instrumental soundtracks from her films, most of which include vocals by Julie). Except where noted otherwise, all were released in the United States. For indexing purposes, the Discography entry number (i.e. **D01**) is listed on the far left side of each entry. It is followed by the name of the recording, then the releasing company and the year of release in parentheses, and finally the manufacturer order number.

D01   _Starlight Roof_ (Columbia Records; 1948) 78/Col (E) - DB- 2400/1

A 78 rpm studio recording by members of the 1947 revue performed at the London Hippodrome. Julie (age 12) sings "I Am Titania." Other cast: Pat Kirkwood, Vic Oliver, chorus. Music and Lyrics: George Melachrino and others. Conductor: Guy Daines.

D02   _The Boy Friend_ (RCA; 1954) RCA LOC-1018

Original Broadway cast recording of Julie's first stage appearance in the U.S, costarring Ann Wakefield and John Hewer. Music and Lyrics: Sandy Wilson. Orchestrations: Ted Royal, Charles l. Cooke. With Paul McGrane and his Bearcats under the direction of Anton Coppola. See **S15** for more information.

Songs include:
Overture (The Bearcats); Perfect Young Ladies (Perfect Young Ladies, Pat Girard); The Boy Friend (Andrews and Ensemble), Fancy Forgetting (Ruth Altman, Eric Berry); Won't You Charleston With Me (Wakefield, Bob Scheerer); I Could Be Happy With You (Andrews, Scheerer); Sur La Plage (Ensemble); A Room in Bloomsbury (Andrews, Hewer); The You Don't Want to Play With Me Blues (Altman, Berry, Perfect Young Ladies); Safety in Numbers (Wakefield, Boyfriends); The Riviera (Wakefield, Scheerer, Ensemble); It's Never Too Late to Fall in Love (Geoffrey Hibbert, Dilys Lay); Carnival Tango (Bearcats); Poor Little Pierette (Andrews, Altman); Finale (Company).

D03   *My Fair Lady* -- Broadway cast (Col; 1956) Col OL-5090

Original Broadway cast recording featuring Julie Andrews, Rex Harrison, Stanley Holloway, Robert Coote, John Michael King, and Phillipa Bevans. Music by Frederick Loewe. Lyrics by Alan Jay Lerner. Orchestrations: Robert Russell Bennet and Philip Jay Lang. Conductor: Franz Allers. See **S16** for more information.

Songs include:
Overture (Orchestra); Why Can't the English (Harrison); Wouldn't it Be Loverly (Andrews and Ensemble); With a Little Bit of Luck (Holloway, Gordon Dilworth, Rod McLennan); I'm an Ordinary Man (Harrison); Just You Wait (Andrews); The Rain in Spain (Andrews, Harrison, Coote); I Could Have Danced All Night (Andrews, Bevans, Maids); Ascot Gavotte (Ensemble); On the Street Where You Live (King); You Did It (Harrison, Coote, Bevans, Household); Show Me (Andrews, King); Get Me to the Church On Time (Holloway, Ensemble); A Hymn to Him (Harrison) Without You (Andrews); I've Grown Accustomed to Her Face (Harrison).

D04   *My Fair Lady* -- London cast (Col; 1956) Col OS-2015

Original London cast recording, with Julie and most of the Broadway principal cast. Betty Wolfe replaced Phillipa Bevans as Mrs. Pearce. Leonard Weir replaced John Michael King as Freddy. Alan Dudley and Bob Chisolm replaced Gordon Dilworth and Rod McLennan as Alfred P. Doolittle's cronies. Same songs as the Broadway version (see **D03**). Conductor: Cyril Orandel. See **S16** for more information.

D05   *High Tor* -- (Decca;1956) Decca DL 8272

Combination studio recording and original soundtrack of the CBS-TV special starring Julie Andrews, Bing Crosby, and Everett Sloane (see **T04**). Music by Arthur Schwartz. Lyrics by Maxwell Anderson. Orchestrations: Joseph J. Lilley.

Songs include:
Living One Day at a Time (Crosby); When You're In Love (Crosby); Sad is the Life of a Sailor's Wife (Andrews); A Little Love, A Little While (Crosby); When You're in Love (Sloane, Andrews); John Barleycorn (Crosby); Once Upon a Long Ago (Andrews, Crosby); John Barleycorn (Crosby, Chorus); A Little Love, A Little While (Reprise by Crosby).

D06   *Cinderella (Col; 1957)* Col OL-5190 and Col OS-2005

Original televsion soundtrack recording of the CBS-TV special (see **T03**), the only musical created by Richard Rogers (music) and Oscar Hammerstein II (lyrics) especially for television. Singing with Julie are Jon Cypher, Edie Adams, Ilka Chase, Kaye Ballard, Alice Ghostley, Dorothy Stickney, and Howard Lindsay.

Songs include:
March: Where is Cinderella? (Orchestra); In My Own Little Corner (Andrews); The Prince is Giving a Ball (Bob Penn, Ensemble); Royal Dressing Room Scene (Stickney, Lindsay, Iggie Wellington, George Hall); In My Own Little Corner (Reprise by Andrews); Godmother's Song: Impossible! It's Possible! (Adams, Andrews); Gavotte (Orchestra); Ten Minutes Ago (Andrews, Cypher); Stepsisters' Lament (Ghostley, Ballard); Waltz For a Ball (Orchestra); Do I Love You Because You're Beautiful (Andrews, Cypher); A Lovely Night (Andrews, Chase, Ballard, Ghostley); The Search (Orchestra); The Wedding (Orchestra)

D07   *The Lass With the Delicate Air*
               (RCA; 1957) RCA LPM-1403 and RCA LSP-1403

D08   *Julie Andrews Sings* **(RCA; 1958) RCA LPM-1681 and LSP-1681**

D09   *Tell It Again* **(Angel; 1958) Angel 65041.**

Julie recites rhymes with Martyn Green.

D10   *Rose-Marie* **(RCA; 1958) RCA LOP 1001 (RD-27143 in England)**

Studio recording of the classic operetta. Other cast: Giorgio Tozzi, Meier Tzelniker, Frances Day, Marion Keene, Frederick Harvey, John Hauxvell, Tudor Evans. Music: Rudolf Friml, Herbert Stothart. Lyrics: Otto Harbach, Oscar Hammerstein II. Conductor: Lehmen Engel.

D11   *Camelot* **(Columbia; 1960) Col OS-8521, CBS-7009, KOS-2031**

Original Broadway cast album featuring Julie, with Richard Burton, Robert Goulet, Roddy McDowall, and Mary Sue Berry. Music by Frederick Loewe. Lyrics by Alan Jay Lerner. Orchestrations: Robert Russell Bennet and Philip Jay Lang. Conductor: Franz Allers. See **S17** for more information.

Songs include:
Overture (Orchestra); I Wonder What the King is Doing Tonight (Burton); The Simple Joys of Maidenhood (Andrews); Camelot (Burton); Follow Me (Berry); Lusty Month of May (Andrews, Ensemble); C'est Moi (Goulet); Take Me to the Fair (Bruce Yarnell, James Gannon, John Cullum); How to Handle a Woman (Burton); If Ever I Would Leave You (Goulet); Parade (Orchestra): Before I Gaze at You Again (Andrews); The Seven Deadly Virtues (McDowall); What Do the Simple Folk Do? (Burton, Andrews); Fie on Goodness (Knights); I Loved You Once in Silence (Andrews); Guenevere (Ensemble); Camelot (Reprise by Burton).

D12   *Broadway's Fair Julie* **(Columbia; 1962) Col CS-8512**

With Henri Rene and his Orchestra.

Songs (and composers) include:
Looking For a Boy (Gershwins); How Long Has This Been Going On (Gershwins); I Feel Pretty (Sondheim/Bernstein); A Sleeping Bee (Arlen/Capote); Baubles, Bangles, and Beads (Wright/Forrest); How are Things in Glocca Mora (Burton/Lane); A Little Bit in Love (Comden/Green/Bernstein); This is New (I. Gershwin; Weill); A Fellow Needs a Girl (Rodgers/Hammerstein); How Can I Wait (Lerner/Loewe); I Didn't Know What Time it Was (Rodgers/Hart); If Love Were All (Coward).

D13   *Don't Go Near the Lion's Cage Tonight* **(Columbia; 1962)**
               Col CS-8686

D14   *Julie and Carol at Carnegie Hall* **(Columbia; 1962) Col OS-2240**

Original soundtrack recording of the CBS-TV television special costarring Julie and Carol Burnett (see **T11**).

Songs (with composers) and skits include:
No Mozart Tonight (Burnett; Mike Nichols/Ken Welch); You're So London (Andrews, Burnett; Nichols/Welch); Oh Dear What Can the Matter Be (Andrews; arr: Welch); From Russia: The Nausiev Ballet (Andrews and Burnett skit including the Irving Berlin songs: There's No Business Like Show Business, The Girl That I Marry, Doin' What Comes Naturally); Meantime (Burnett; Stillman/Allen); From Switzerland: The Pratt Family (Andrews and Burnett skit including original songs by Nichols/Welch: Pratt Family Tree, The Things We Like Best, Ding Dong Yum Yum); History of Musical Comedy medley (Andrews, Burnett; songs listed below); From Texas: Big D (Andrews, Burnett; Loesser).

History of Musical Comedy medley includes:
Every Little Movement; Ah! Sweet Mystery of Life; Tramp, Tramp, Tramp; Look For the Silver Lining; Limehouse Blues; Funny Face; Fidgety feet; 'S Wonderful; Lucky Day; Hallelujah; I Get a Kick Out of You; Night and Day; Where or When; Yesterdays; I Cain't Say No; Wouldn't it Be Loverly; A Boy Like That; I Have a Love

D15   *Mary Poppins* **(Buena Vista; 1964) BV-4026, ST-4026**

Original soundtrack recording of Julie's film debut for Walt Disney (see **F01**). Co-starring Dick Van Dyke, David Tomlinson, Glynis Johns, Ed Wynn, Karen Dotrice, Matthew Garber. Winner of a 1965 Grammy for Best Children's Recording. Oscar wins for best score, best song ("Chim Chim Cher-ee"), nomination for score adaptation or treatment. Music and lyrics by Richard M. Sherman and Robert B. Sherman. Orchestrations and conducting by Irwin Kostal.

Songs include:
Overture (Orchestra and Chorus); The Perfect Nanny (Dotrice, Garber); Sister Suffragette (Johns); The Life I Lead (Tomlinson); A Spoonful of Sugar (Andrews); Pavement Artist/Chim Chim Cheree (Van Dyke); Jolly Holliday (Van Dyke; Andrews); Super-cali-fragi-listic-expial-a-docious (Van Dyke, Andrews, Pearlies); Stay Awake (Andrews); I Love to Laugh (Wynn, Van Dyke, Andrews); A British Bank/The Life I Lead (Tomlinson, Andrews); Feed the Birds (Andrews, Chorus); Fidelity Fiduciary Bank; Chim Chim Cheree (Van Dyke, Andrews, Dotrice, Garber); Step in Time (Van Dyke, Chimney Sweeps); A Man Has Dreams/The Life I Lead/A Spoonful of Sugar (Tomlinson/Van Dyke); Let's Go Fly a Kite (Tomlinson, Van Dyke, Londoners)

D16   *The Americanization of Emily* **(Reprise; 1964) RS-6151**

Original film soundtrack recording. Music by Johnny Mandel. No songs by Julie. Includes the Johnny Mercer/Mandel song "Emily," sung by Jack Jones, plus instrumental tracks from the film. See **F02** for more information.

D17   *The Sound of Music* **(RCA; 1965) RCA LSOD-2005**

Original film soundtrack recording, featuring Julie, Bill Lee (dubbed for Christopher Plummer), Dan Truhitte, Charmian Carr, Marjorie McKay (dubbed for Peggy Wood). Score by Richard Rogers (music) and Oscar Hammerstein II (lyrics). Orchestrations and conducting by Irwin Kostal. Grammy Award nominee for Album of the Year. Oscar win for Best Score Adaptation or treatment. See **F03** for more information.

Songs include:
Prelude/The Sound of Music (Andrews); Overture and Preludium (Orchestra and Nun's Chorus); Morning Hymn and Alleluia (Nun's Chorus); Maria (Nun's Chorus, including Marni Nixon); I Have Confidence (Andrews); Sixteen Going On Seventeen (Carr, Truhitte); My Favorite Things (Andrews); Climb Every Mountain (McKay); The Lonely Goatherd (Andrews, Children); Something Good (Andrews, Lee); Processional and Maria (Organ, Orchestra, Nun's Chorus), Edelweiss (Andrews, Lee, Children, Chorus); So Long Farewell (Children); Climb Every Mountain (Orchestra, Chorus)

D18   *Firestone Presents Your Favorite Christmas Carols, Vol. 5, Starring Julie Andrews* **(Firestone; 1966) Firestone SLP-7012 or MLP-7012**

Features Julie singing Christmas Carols, acommpanied by Andre Previn conducting the Firestone Orchestra and Chorus.

Songs include:
Joy to the World, Irish Carol, O Little Town of Bethlehem, Deck the Halls, Angels From the Realms, Away in a Manger, The Bells of Christmas, It Came Upon the Midnight Clear, Sunny Bank (I Saw Three Ships), God Rest You Merry Gentlemen, Wexford Carol, Jingle Bells

D19   *Torn Curtain* **(Decca; 1966) Decca DL-79155**

Original soundtrack recording of the instrumental film score, composed by John Addison. See **F04** for more information.

D20   *Hawaii* **(UA; 1966) UA-LA283**

Original film soundtrack featuring a score by Elmer Bernstein. Julie sings the Academy award-nominated "My Wishing Doll" (music by Bernstein, lyrics by Hal David). See **F05** for more information.

D21   *Torn Curtain* **(WB; 1966) WB BSK-3185; WB FMC 10**

This was the first score to be composed for the Hitchcock film, but was replaced by John Addison's score in the released version (see **D19**). This first score was composed by Alfred Hitchcock's long-time collaborator Bernard Herrman, who ended their 10-year professional relationship when they disagreed on the style of score required for the film. Conducted by Elmer Bernstein, with the Royal Philharmonic Orchestra.

Tracks include:
Prelude, The Radiogram, The Phone -- The Bookstore, Valse Lente, The Travel Desk -- Gromek, The Farmhouse, The Body, The Killing, The Toast -- The Photos, The

Cab Driver -- The Hill, Discovery -- The Blackboard, The Formula -- The Corridor, the Bicycles -- The Bus, Prelude (Reprise).

D22   ***Thoroughly Modern Millie***
             (Decca; 1967) Dec DL 71500; Brunswick STA-8685.

Original film soundtrack recording, featuring Julie, Carol Channing, James Fox, John Gavin, Ann Dee. Original songs by Sammy Cahn and Jimmy Van Heusen. Other 1920s songs by various composers. Musical score by Elmer Bernstein. Orchestration and conducting by Andre Previn and Joseph Gershenson. Oscar win for Best Score Adaptation or Treatment, nominees for original score and title song. See **F06**.

Songs include:
Prelude/Thoroughly Modern Millie (Andrews); Overture (Orchestra); Jimmy (Andrews); The Tapioca (Fox, Orchestra; Dialogue: Andrews, Fox)) ; Jazz Baby (Channing); Jewish Wedding Song: Trinkt Le Chaim (Andrews); Intermission Medley (Andrews); Poor Butterfly (Andrews; Dialogue: Andrews, Gavin) Rose of Washington Square (Dee); Baby Face (Andrews); Do It Again (Channing); Reprise: Thoroughly Modern Millie (Andrews); Exit Music (Orchestra).

D23   ***Star!*** **(20th Century-Fox; 1968) 20th DS-5102**

Original film soundtrack recording, featuring Julie, Daniel Massey, Bruce Forsyth, and Beryl Reid. Title song by Sammy Cahn, Jimmy Van Heusen. Other songs, music, and material by Saul Chaplin, Walter Williams, Bruce Siever, Paul Morande, J. P. Long, Maurice Scott, Noel Coward, Bud deSylva, Gus Kahn, Al Jolson, William Hargreaves, Philip Braham, Douglas Furber, Ira and George Gershwin, Cole Porter, and Kurt Weill. Score arrangement orchestration by Lennie Hayton. Oscar nominations for title song, score adaptation See **F08** for more information.

Songs (and composers) include:
Overture (Orchestra); Star! (Andrews; Cahn/Van Heusen); Piccadilly (Andrews, Forsyth, Reid; Williams/Sievers/Morande); In My Garden of Joy (The Daffodils; Chaplin) Oh, it's a Lovely War (Andrews, Daffodils; Long/Scott); 'N Everything (Garret Lewis; De Sylva/Kahn/Jolson); Burlington Bertie From Bow (Andrews; Hargreaves); Parisian Pierrot (Andrews; Coward); Limehouse Blues (Andrews, Male Chorus; Brahm/Furber); Someone to Watch Over Me (Andrews; Gershwins); Dear Little Boy...Dear Little Girl (Andrews, Massey; Gershwins); Has Anybody Seen Our Ship? (Andrews, Massey; Coward); Someday I'll Find You (Andrews; Coward); The Physician (Andrews, Girls; Porter); My Ship (Andrews; Weill/I. Gershwin); Jenny (Andrews; Weill/I. Gershwin).

D24   ***Darling Lili*** **(RCA Victor; 1970) RCA LSPX-1000**

Studio recording of music and songs from the film (see **F09**), featuring Julie, Gloria Paul, and the Henry Mancini Orchestra and Chorus. Among other songs, Julie sings the Academy award-nominated "Whistling Away the Dark." Curiosities: The charming World War medley that Julie sings in the film is not included on this album. The title song, performed on the album by Mancini's Orchestra and Chorus, is not heard in the release version of the film.

Songs include:
Overture (Orchestra, Chorus); Whistling Away the Dark (Andrews); The Little Birds (Les P'tits Oiseanux) by the Le Lysee Francais de Los Angeles Children's Choir; The Girl in No Man's Land (Andrews); Gypsy Violin (Orchestra); I'll Give You Three

Guesses (Andrews); Darling Lili (Orchestra , Chorus); Smile Away Each Rainy Day (Andrews); The Can-Can Cafe (Orchestra); Reprise: I'll Give You Three Guesses (Andrews); Skal: Let's Have Another on Me (Orchestra, Chorus); Your Good Will Ambassador (Gloria Paul); Reprise: Whistling Away the Dark (Andrews).

D25   *A Little Bit in Love* **(Harmony; 1970) H-30021, CHM-687**

Songs include: A Little Bit in Love (Comden/Green/Bernstein); I Feel Pretty (Sondheim/Bernstein); How Can I Wait (Lerner/Loewe), Burlington Bertie From Bow (Hargreaves); If Love Were All (Coward); This is New (I. Gershwin/Weill); Waiting At the Church (Leigh/Pether); Looking For a Boy (Gershwins); By the Light of the Silvery Moon (Madden/Edwards).

D26   *Julie and Carol at Lincoln Centre* **(Columbia; 1971) Col S-31153**

Original soundtrack recording of the CBS-TV special (see **T24**), reuniting Julie and Carol Burnett. Original material by Ken and Mitzi Welch.

Songs (and composers) include: Opening/Our Classy Classical Show (Welchs); Girls in the Band (Welches); Madame Abernall's (K. Welch); I Could Have Danced All Night (Lerner/Loewe); He's Gone Away (K. Welch); Medley of the 60s (see below for complete list of songs); Wait Till the Sun Shines Nellie (Sterling/ Van Tilzer); Finale.

Medley of the 60's includes: Sgt. Pepper's Lonely Hearts Club Band; With a Little Help from My Friends; The Beat Goes On; I Dig Rock and Roll Music; Everybody's Talkin'; Gentle On My Mind; Witchita Lineman; Little Green Apples; Honey; Both Sides Now; If; Up Up and Away, Do You Know the Way to San Jose?; By the Time I Get to Phoenix; Downtown; Feelin' Groovy; Sunny; Raindrops Keep Fallin' From My Head; You've Made Me So Very Happy; The Girl From Ipanema; This Girl's in Love With You; Georgy Girl; Hello Dolly; Sesame Street; Moon River; People; Eleanor Rigby; What the World Needs Now is Love; Come Together; Put Your Hand in the Hand; Let it Be; And When I Die; We Shall Overcome; Aquarius; Son of a Preacherman; What Kind of Fool Am I; I'll Never Fall in Love Again; Alfie; What Now My Love; Goin' Out Of My Head; Born Free; Strangers in the Night; (Where Do I Begin) Love Story; It Must Be Him; A Spoonful of Sugar; Spinning Wheel; Is That All There Is?

D27   *TV's Fair Julie* **(Harmony; 1972) Harmony KJ-31958**

Reissue of *Broadway's Fair Julie* to coincide with Julie's 1972 ABC-TV series.

D28   **The World of Julie Andrews**
            (Columbia; 1972) Col KG-31970, CBS-68234

Called *The Best of Julie Andrews* in Great Britian. Reissue of songs from *Broadway's Fair Julie* (**D12**), *Don't Go Near the Lion's Cage Tonight* (**D13**), and the London cast recording of *My Fair Lady* (**D04**).

D29   *Secret of Christmas* **(Embassy/CBS; 1972) Embassy 31237, 31522**

Released in England only.

D30 *Julie Andrews* (RCA; 1975) RCA-ANL-1-1098; RCA HY-1002

A reissue of songs from *Lass With the Delicate Air* (**D08**) and *Julie Andrews Sings* (**D07**).

D31 *The Pink Panther Strikes Again* (UA; 1976) UA LA-694-G

Original film soundtrack recording. Score by Henry Mancini. Julie sings "Until You Love Me" in a man's voice. (She did not appear in the film, but her voice was used.)

D32 *An Evening with Julie Andrews* (RCA; 1977) RCA SX-281 (A-7)

Released in Japan only.

D33 *Broadway Magic, Best of the Great Broadway Musicals*
(Columbia; 1977) Col JSA-36282.

Collection of songs from original Broadway cast recordings includes Julie singing "I Could Have Danced All Night," with Betty Wolfe (from *My Fair Lady*).

D34 *Broadway Magic, Vol.2, Great Performances*
(Columbia; 1978) Col JSA-36409.

Collection of songs from original Broadway cast recordings includes Julie singing "The Rain in Spain" from *My Fair Lady* (with Rex Harrison and Robert Coote) and "What Do the Simple Folk Do?" from *Camelot* (with Richard Burton).

D35 *Magic Moments from the Music of Rodgers and Hammerstein*
(GRT Music; 1978) 9DM-8

Four-record set featuring various artists performing the music of Rodgers and Hammerstein in studio recordings, movie soundtracks, or original stage cast recordings. Julie sings "Do Re Mi" and the title song from *The Sound of Music* soundtrack. Julie and Jon Cypher sing "Do I Love You Because You're Beautiful?" from the soundtrack of the CBS-TV *Cinderella* special.

D36 *10* (Warner; 1979) WB BSK 3399

Original film soundtrack recording, featuring Julie, Dudley Moore, and the Henry Mancini Orchestra and Chorus. Score is by Henry Mancini, with the exception of Ravel's "Bolero." Julie sings "He Pleases Me" (solo) and the Academy award-nominated Mancini song "It's Easy to Say," first as a duet with Dudley Moore and later as a solo. Other instrumental and/or choral selections: "Don't Call It Love," "Get it On," "Keyboard Harmony," "The Hot Sand Mexican Band," "Something For Jenny," and "I Have an Ear For Love." See **F12** for more information.

D37 *Victor/Victoria* (MGM/Polygram; 1982) MG-1-5407

Original film soundtrack recording, featuring Julie Andrews, Robert Preston, Lesley Ann Warren, and the Henry Mancini Orchestra and Chorus. Oscar-nominated score is by Henry Mancini (music) and Leslie Bricusse (lyrics). See **F15** for more information.

Songs include: Main Title: Crazy World (Orchestra); You and Me (Andrews, Preston); The Shady Dame from Seville (Andrews); Alone in Paris (Orchestra); King's Can Can (Orchestra); Le Jazz Hot (Andrews); Crazy World (Andrews); Chicago, Illinois (Warren); Cat and Mouse (Orchestra); You and Me (Orchestra); Gay Paree (Preston); Finale (Orchestra).

D38   *Love Me Tender* (Baunbridge Records; 1982) **BT-6260**

Julie sings Country-and-Western songs.

Songs include:
Crazy; Some Days are Diamonds; See the Funny Little Clown; When I Dream; (Hey Won't You Play) Another Somebody Done Me Wrong Song; Love Me Tender (with Johnny Cash); I Wish I Could Hurt That Way Again; The Valley That Time Forgot; Blanket on the Ground; Love is a Place Where Two People Fall.

D39   *Love, Julie*
             (USA Records; January, 1988) Contact: USA Records; Burbank, CA

Produced by Robert Wells. According to an article by Larry Kart, in the *Chicago Tribune* (1/24/88), Julie made this album as a birthday gift for husband, Blake Edwards, along with her pal Wells, and Edwards subsequently persuaded her to release it commercially. Arriving five years after her last album was released, this album has generated some mixed reviews. In *People* (1/25/88), David Hiltbrand called it "a curious patchwork outing, sometimes stately and soothing, just as often exasperating...Not that anything is wrong with her voice...The problem is that stiff upper lip." In Larry Kart's *Chicago Tribune* (1/29/88) review of Julie's January, 1988, concert appearance in Chicago, Kart said that in the album Julie sings with "a caressing intimacy and warmth."

Songs include:
Out of This World; Come Rain, Come Shine; Love; Tea For Two; How Deep is the Ocean; My Lucky Day; The Island; A Soundsketch; So In Love; Where or When; What Are You Doing the Rest of Your Life?; Nobody Does it Better; Nobody Does it Better (reprise)

D40   *Time/Life Treasury of Christmas* (**Time/Life Records;
             October, 1988) Order: Time/Life Music (Richmond, VA)**

Two-volume set of Christmas songs by various performers includes Julie singing *God Rest Ye Merry Gentlemen*, *Joy to the World*, and *Irish Carol*.

Bibliography

B01   "49 Turning 50." *50 Plus*, 5/85.
        Photo of Julie.

B02   Adler, Renata. *Year in the Dark, A*. New York: Berkley Publishers, 1969.
        Collection of film reviews includes Adler's *Star!* film review from the *New York Times*.

B03   "AFI Life Achievement Award: A Salute to Jack Lemmon." *Variety*, 5/31/88.
        Review of the CBS-TV special hosted by Julie.

B04   "AFI Life Achievement Award: A Salute to Jack Lemmon." *TV Guide*, 5/28/88.
        Commentary on CBS-TV special hosted by Julie.

B05   Aleysworth, Thomas G. *History of Movie Musicals*. New York: Gallery Books, 1978.

B06   Amory, Cleveland. Review of *The Julie Andrews Hour* (her ABC-TV series). *TV Guide*, 10/26/72.

B07   Andrews, Julie. "My Friend, Carol Burnett." *Good Housekeeping*, 1/72.

B08   Barrenburg, Bruce. *Star!* film review. *Evening News* (Newark, NJ), 10/23/68.

B09   *Beller, Miles*. "AFI Life Achievement Award: A Salute to Jack Lemmon." *Hollywood Reporter*, 5/31/88.
        Review of the CBS-TV special hosted by Julie.

B10   *Beller, Miles*. "Julie Andrews: The Sound of Christmas." *Hollywood Reporter*, 2/16/87.
        Review of the ABC-TV special starring Julie.

B11   Bennetts, Leslie. "Julie Andrews: Prim and Improper." *New York Times*, 3/14/82.

B12   Bergan, Ronald. *The United Artists Story*. New York: Crown Publishers, 1986.
Panoramic history of United Artists films includes brief discussion of *Hawaii*.

B13   Blum, Daniel. *A Pictorial History of the American Theatre: 1860-1970*. New York: Crown Publishers, 1969 and 1971.
Photos and brief discussions of Julie's three Broadway musical appearances.

B14   Blum, Daniel. *Screen World* (1964-1968 editions). New York: Macmillan, 1964-1968.
Includes cast and crew data on Julie's films released during this period.

B15   Blum, Daniel. *Theatre World, 1954-55 and 1955-56*. New York: Macmillan, 1956 and 1957.
Includes cast and crew data on Broadway's *The Boy Friend* and *My Fair Lady*.

B16   Bookbinder, Robert. *Films of the 70s*. Secacus, NJ: Citadel Press, 1982.
Includes a discussion and synopsis of Julie's film *10* (1979).

B17   Bordman, Gerald. *American Musical Theatre: A Chronicle*. New York: Oxford University Press, 1977.
Brief discussions of Julie's three Broadway musical appearances.

B18   Bordman, Gerald. *The Oxford Companion to American Theatre*. New York and Oxford: Oxford University Press, 1984.
Brief discussion of Julie's Broadway appearances.

B19   Brode, Douglas. *Films of the 60s*. Secacus, NJ: Citadel Press, 1980.
Includes discussions and synopses of Julie's films *Mary Poppins* (1964) and *The Sound of Music* (1965).

B20   Bronner, Edwin J. *The Encyclopedia of the American Theatre*. San Diego, CA: A.S. Barnes, 1980.

B21   Brooks, Tim and Earle Marsh. *The Complete Directory to Prime Time Network TV Shows, 1946-Present*. New York: Ballantine Books, 1979.
Includes short description of the 1972-73 ABC-TV *Julie Andrews Hour*.

B22   Brooks, Tim. *The Complete Directory to Prime Time TV Stars, 1946-Present*. New York: Ballantine Books, 1987.
Includes short biographical sketch of Julie.

B23   Brown, Peter H. *The Real Oscar*. Westport, CT: Arlington House, 1977.
Book about behind-the-scenes Oscar occurrences implies that Julie's career was doomed when she won an Oscar for the saccharine role of Mary Poppins.

B24   Brown, Peter H. and Jim Pinkston. *Oscar Dearest.* New York: Harper & Row, 1987.
Mean-spirited, exploitative book about Oscar "scandal, politics, and greed" discusses the effect of Julie's *Mary Poppins* Oscar on her film career.

B25   Canby, Vincent. *Victor/Victoria* film reviews. *New York Times,* 3/19/82 and 4/4/82.

B26   Candee, Marjorie Devit. *Current Biography Yearbook, 1956.* New York: H. W. Wilson, 1956.
Includes short biographical sketch on Julie.

B27   Chase, C. "Julie Andrews Fights Back." *McCall's,* 5/73.

B28   Chase, Chris. "Real Life Buoys *That's Life.*" *New York Times,* 9/21/86.

B29   Christy, G. "New Life of Julie Andrews." *Good Housekeeping,* 5/70.

B30   Chunovic, Louis. "Broadcast TV Museum Fete to Honor Andrews, Gelbart." *Hollywood Reporter,* 2/18/88.
Story about Los Angeles chapter of Museum of Broadcasting honoring Julie and writer Larry Gelbart in a May 1988 festival, including a screening of Julie's 1962 TV special, *Julie and Carol at Carnegie Hall,* costarring Carol Burnett.

B31   *Cinema Star Album: Julie Andrews.* Seattle, WA: Cinema Posts by Post, 1980.
This 184-page softcover book features both black-and-white and color photos of Julie. Written and published in Japan, it is one of a series on various celebrities.

B32   Cottrell, John. *The Unauthorized Life Story of a Super Star: Julie Andrews.* New York: Dell, 1968.
Fan-magazine type paperbook merchandised to take advantage of Julie's popularity. It, nevertheless, includes much more detailed coverage of Julie's early years in England than does the better-known Robert Windeler hardback biography (see entry **B185**).

B33   Cover article. *TV Guide,* 5/22/65.

B34   Crosby, John. Review of *Rodgers and Hammerstein's Cinderella,* CBS-TV special starring Julie. *New York Herald-Tribune,* 4/1/57.

B35   Crowther, Bosley. "Where Are the Women?" *New York Times,* 1/23/86.

B36   Denby, David. *Film 70/71.* New York; Simon and Schuster, 1971.
Includes Arthur Knight's review of *Darling Lili* from *Saturday Review.*

B37   Droesch, Paul. Commentary on *Julie Andrews: The Sound of Christmas,* ABC TV special. *TV Guide,* 12/11/87.

B38   Druxman, Michael B. *One Good Film Deserves Another: A Pictorial History of Film Sequels.* New York: A.S. Barnes, 1977.
Includes a discussion and synopsis of Julie's movie *Hawaii* (1966).

B39   *Duet For One* film review. *American Film,* 12/86.

B40   *Duet For One* film review. *Commonwealth*, 3/13/87.

B41   *Duet For One* film review. *Los Angeles*, 2/87.

B42   *Duet For One* film review. *MacLean's*, 3/2/87.

B43   *Duet For One* film review. *People*, 3/2/87.

B44   *Duet For One* film review. *Philadelphia*, 4/87.

B45   *Duet For One* film review. *Playboy*, 2/87.

B46   *Duet For One* film review. *Time*, 3/2/87.

B47   Dunne, John Gregory. *The Studio*. New York: Bantam Books, 1973.

B48   Eames, John Douglas. *The MGM Story*. New York: Crown Publishers, 1975, 1979, and 1985.
　　　　Panoramic history of MGM films includes brief discussions of *The Americanization of Emily* and *Victor/Victoria*.

B49   Eames, John Douglas. *The Paramount Story*. New York: Crown Publishers, 1985.
　　　　Panoramic history of Paramount films includes brief discussions of *Darling Lili* and *S.O.B.*

B50   Edwards, Julie. *The Last of the Really Great Whangdoodles*. New York: Harper & Row, 1974.
　　　　Julie's second book (penned under her married name). See Appendix C for more information.

B51   Edwards, Julie. *Mandy*. New York: Harper & Row, 1971.
　　　　Julie's first book (penned under her married name). See Appendix C for more information.

B52   Ellis, Jack C., Charles Derry, and Sharon Kern. *Film Book Bibliography, 1940-1975*. Jefferson, NC: McFarland and Co., 1988.

B53   Ewen, David. *American Musical Theatre*. New York: Holt, Rinehart, and Winston, 1958, 1959, and 1970.
　　　　Analytical history of major American musicals includes insightful commentary on the steps leading up to the creation of the original Broadway productions of *My Fair Lady and Camelot* (starring Julie), and *The Sound of Music* (starring Mary Martin).

B54   Eyles, Allen and Pat Billings. *Hollywood Today*. New York: A. S. Barnes, 1971.
　　　　Dictionary-style biographies of 370 creative film talents, including Julie.

B55   Fitzgerald, Michael G. *Universal Pictures: A Panoramic History in Words, Pictures, and Filmographies*. Westport, CT: Arlington House, 1975.

B56   Franks, Don. *Tony, Grammy, Emmy, Country: A Broadway, Television, and Records Awards Reference*. Jefferson, NC: McFarland and Co., 1986.

B57   Gittelson, N. "Julie and Her Family." *McCall's*, 11/86.

B58   Gottfried, Marvin. *Broadway Musicals*. New York: Harry N. Abrams, Inc., 1982.
Discussions of Julie's three Broadway musical appearances.

B59   Gould, Jack. Review of CBS-TV special, *Julie and Carol at Carnegie Hall*. *New York Times*, 6/12/62.

B60   Graham, Shelah. *Confessions of a Hollywood Columnist*. New York: Bantam, 1969.
Gossipy book about various Hollywood celebrities, including Julie.

B61   Greenspun, Roger. *Darling Lili* film review. *New York Times*, 8/9/70.

B62   Hadded-Garcia, G. "Thoroughly Modern Julie Andrews." *McCall's*, 1/88 and 2/88.

B63   Hanson, Stephen L. *S.O.B.* film review. *Magill's Cinema Annual, 1982*. Englewood Cliffs, NJ: Salem Press, 1983.

B64   Harris, Radie. "Broadway Ballyhoo" (column). *Hollywood Reporter*, 7/23/68.
Report on London world premiere of *Star!* (unattended by Julie).

B65   Harris, Radie. "Broadway Ballyhoo" (column). *Hollywood Reporter*, 11/30/87.
Columnist attends special screening of Julie's Christmas 1987 ABC-TV special, *The Sound of Christmas*.

B66   Harris, Steve. *Film, Television, and Stage Music on Phonograph Records*. Jefferson, NC: McFarland and Co., 1988.
Includes data on several of Julie's recordings.

B67   Hartroll, Phyllis. *The Oxford Companion to Theatre*. New York and Oxford: Oxford University Press, 1983.
Brief discussions of Julie's Broadway appearances.

B68   Hawkins, William. Theatre review of *My Fair Lady*. *New York World-Telegram*, 3/16/56.

B69   Herbert, Jan. *Who's Who in the Theatre*, 17th Edition. Detroit, MI: Gale Research, 1981.
Brief biographical sketch of Julie.

B70   Higham, Charles. *Celebrity Circus*. New York: Dell, 1979
Collection of celebrity articles includes a reprint of Higham's *New York Times* article about Julie. (See next entry.)

B71   Higham, Charles. "The Rise and Fall...and Rise of Julie Andrews." *New York Times*, 8/21/77.

B72   Hiltbrand, David. Review of *Love, Julie* record album. *People*, 1/25/88.
See *Discography* entry **D39** for comments on this uncomplimentary review.

B73   Hirschhorn, Clive. *The Hollywood Musical*. New York: Crown Publishers, 1981.

B74 Hirschhorn, Clive. *The Universal Story*. New York: Crown Publishers, 1983.
Panoramic history of Universal Studio films includes brief discussions of *Torn Curtain, Thoroughly Modern Millie*, and *Little Miss Marker*.

B75 Holden, Steven. "For Julie Andrews, the Sound of a Different Music." *New York Times*, 11/17/87.
Interview with Julie prior to her appearance at Long Island's Westbury Music Fair during her late 1987 concert tour.

B76 Hummel, David. *The Collector's Guide to the American Musical Theatre, Vols. I and II*. Metuchen, NJ: Scarecrow Press, 1984.

B77 Interview and cover featuring Julie. *Los Angeles*, 12/86.

B78 Jackson, Arthur. *The Best Musicals*. New York: Crown Publishers, 1978.

B79 "Julie and Her Family." *McCall's*, 11/86.

B80 "Julie Andrews: The Sound of Christmas." *Variety*, 12/18/87.
Review of her December, 1987, ABC-TV special.

B81 "Julie Plays Gertie." *Look*, 9/19/67.
Photo story on the filming of *Star!*

B82 Kaplan, Mike. *Variety Presents the Complete Book of Major U.S. Show Business Awards*. New York: Garland Publishing, 1985.
Includes listings of all Tony (Broadway theatre), Grammy (records), Oscar (films), and Emmy (television) nominations and/or wins for Julie.

B83 Kaplan, Philip J. *The Best, Worst, and Most Unusual Hollywood Musicals*. Skokie, IL: Publications, Int'l., 1982.

B84 Kart, Larry. "Chanteuse on the Loose." *Chicago Sun-Times*, 1/24/88.
General interview with Julie on the occasion of her 1987-1988 concert tour.

B85 Kart, Larry. Review of Julie's January 1988 concert appearance in Chicago. *Chicago Sun-Times*, 1/29/88.

B86 Kerr, Walter. Theatre review of *Camelot*. *New York Herald-Tribune*, 2/5/60.

B87 "Last of the Really Great Whangdoodles, The." *Publisher's Weekly*, 5/22/74.
Review of Julie's children's book.

B88 Lawrenson, H. "Sweet Julie." *Esquire*, 1/69.

B89 "Lerner and Loewe, Broadway's Last Romantics." *TV Guide*, 3/12/88.
Commentary on PBS special featuring Julie.

B90 Likeness, George. *The Oscar People*. W. Nenola IL: Wayside Press, 1965.
Discussion of the careers of Oscar-winners, including Julie.

B91 Lloyd, Ann. *Movies of the Seventies*. London: Orbis, 1984.
A discussion of Julie's film *10* (1979) is included.

B92   Lloyd, Ann. *Movies of the Sixties*. London: Orbis, 1983.
        The section on musicals discusses various Julie Andrews films.

B93   Lyle, Joe. "Julie Andrews: I Married a Man Who Didn't Want Me."
        Photoplay, 5/65.
        Interview with Julie regarding her relationship with her husband, Tony
        Walton.

B94   MacDonald, Dwight. *On Movies*. New York: Berkley Publishers, 1969.
        Collection of film reviews includes *The Sound of Music*.

B95   Mahoney, John. *Star!* film review. *Hollywood Reporter*, 7/23/68.

B96   Maltin, Leonard. *The Disney Films*. New York: Crown Publishers, 1972.
        Includes commentary on *Mary Poppins*.

B97   "Mandy." Review of Julie's children's book. *Publisher's Weekly*, 12/13/71.

B98   "Mandy." Review of Julie's children's book. *Time*, 12/27/71.

B99   "Many Roles of Julie Andrews, The." *Reader's Digest*, 11/85.

B100   Marchak, Alice and Linda Hunter. *The Supersecs: Behind the Scenes with
        Secretaries of the Superstars*. North Hollywood, CA: Charles Publishing,
        1975.
        Secretaries of Marlon Brando and Julie tell what it's like to be a
        Hollywood secretary.

B101   *Mary Poppins* videocassette film review. *New York Times*, 3/2/86.

B102   *Mary Poppins* videocassette film review. *Parent's*, 11/85.

B103   Maslin, Janet *S.O.B.* film review. *New York Times*, 8/16/81.

B104   McDowall, Roddy. *Double Exposure*. New York: Delcarte Publishers,
        1966.
        Includes a laudatory profile of Julie written by Alan Jay Lerner.

B105   McLeese, Don. Review of Julie's January 1988 concert appearance in
        Chicago. *Chicago Sun-Times*, 1/29/88.

B106   Michael, Paul and James Robert Parish. *The Great American Movie Book*.
        Englewood Cliffs, NJ: Prentice-Hall, 1980.

B107   Michaelson, Judith. "Andrews...Still a Fair Lady." *Los Angeles Times*,
        8/9/84.

B108   Miller, Edwin. *Seventeen Interviews: Film Stars and Superstars*. New
        York: Macmillan, 1970.
        Interviews of celebrities from the pages of *Seventeen* Magazine
        include Julie Andrews.

B109   "Ms. Andrews is No Longer Mary Poppins." *New York Times*, 2/20/87.

B110   Murphy-Martell, Morna. Review of Julie's Long Island, New York, concert
        opening performance. *Hollywood Reporter*, 12/2/87.

B111   Nash, Jay Robert and Stanley Ralph Ross. *Motion Picture Guide,
        1927-1983. Volume I.* Chicago: Cinebooks Inc., 1985.
          Film review of *The Americanization of Emily.*

B112   Nash, Jay Robert and Stanley Ralph Ross. *Motion Picture Guide,
        1927-1983. Volume II.* Chicago: Cinebooks Inc., 1985.
          Film review of *Darling Lili.*

B113   Nash, Jay Robert and Stanley Ralph Ross. *Motion Picture Guide,
        1927-1983. Volume IV.* Chicago: Cinebooks Inc., 1985.
          Film review of *Hawaii.*

B114   Nash, Jay Robert and Stanley Ralph Ross. *Motion Picture Guide,
        1927-1983. Volume V.* Chicago: Cinebooks Inc., 1986.
          Film reviews of *Little Miss Marker, The Man Who Loved Women*, and
        Mary Poppins.

B115   Nash, Jay Robert and Stanley Ralph Ross. *Motion Picture Guide,
        1927-1983. Volume VII.* Chicago: Cinebooks Inc., 1986.
          Film reviews of *S.O.B., The Sound of Music*, and *Star!* Commentary
        on Julie's animated film, *The Singing Princess.*

B116   Nash, Jay Robert and Stanley Ralph Ross. *Motion Picture Guide,
        1927-1983. Volume VIII.* Chicago: Cinebooks Inc., 1987.
          Film reviews of *10, The Tamarind Seed, Thoroughly Modern Millie,
        Torn Curtain,* and *Victor/Victoria.*

B117   Nash, Jay Robert and Stanley Ralph Ross. *Motion Picture Guide,
        1987 Annual.* Chicago: Cinebooks Inc., 1987.
          Film reviews of *Duet For One* and *That's Life!*

B118   Newquist, Roy. *Showcase.* New York: Morrow, 1966.
          Interviews with many celebrities, including Julie.

B119   *Notable Names in the American Theatre.* New York: James T. White and
        Co., 1976.

B120   "Now and Future Queen, The." *Time*, 12/23/64.
          Cover story.

B121   O'Connor, John J. "For Holiday, Puppets, Songs, and Capote Story
        [Truman Capote]." *New York Times*, 12/16/87.

B122   Osborne, Jerry. *Movie/TV Soundtracks and Original Cast Albums Price
        Guide.* Phoenix, AZ: O'Sullivan, Woodside, and Co, 1979.

B123   Osborne, Robert. *Academy Awards Oscar Annual* (1966-1976 volumes). La
        Habra, CA: ESE California, 1966-1976.
          Include discussions of Julie's Oscar-winning films from this time
        period.

B124   Osborne, Robert. "Rambling Reporter" (column). *Hollywood Reporter*,
        10/8/87.
          Julie turns down an invitation from 20th Century-Fox president Rupert
        Murdoch to appear in China to kick off *Sound of Music's* debut on Chinese
        TV.

B125   Osborne, Robert. "Rambling Reporter" (column). *Hollywood Reporter*, 11/20/87.
Brief report of successful opening of Julie's concert tour at Westbury Music Fair in Long Island, New York.

B126   Osborne, Robert. "Rambling Reporter" (column). *Hollywood Reporter*, 1/26/88.
Brief report of Minneapolis extension of Julie's concert tour.

B127   "Over 40 and Fabulous." *Harper's Bazaar*, 9/82.

B128   Palmer, Scott. *British Film Actors' Credits, 1895-1987*. London: Palmer, 1988.

B129   Peary, Daniel. *Close-Ups: The Movie Star Book*. New York: Workman, 1979.
Short articles about celebrities, including one on Julie: "A Talk With a Flickering Star" by Linda Gross.

B130   *Phonolog Reports*. San Diego, CA: Phonolog Publishing Division, 1988.

B131   Pitts, Michael R. and Louis H. Harrison. *Hollywood on Record: The Film Stars' Discography*. Metuchen, NJ: Scarecrow Press, 1978.

B132   *Placido Domingo and Friends*. *Variety*, 8/20/86
Review of a concert held in Universal Amphitheatre in Hollywood to benefit victims of the 1986 Mexico earthquake. Julie was featured, along with other guests. (See *Stage Appearances* **[S49]** for more details.)

B133   Plans for Andrews Christmas special. *Variety*, 8/5/87.

B134   "Playboy Interview: Julie Andrews and Blake Edwards." *Playboy*, 12/82.

B135   "Portrait of a Pioneer." *Dance* Magazine, 7/85.

B136   Quirk, Lawrence J. *The Complete Films of William Holden*. Secaucus, NJ: Citadel Press, 1973 and 1986.
Includes a chapter discussing *S.O.B.*, the 1981 Blake Edwards/Julie Andrews collaboration that turned out to be Holden's last film.

B137   Raymond, Jack. *Show Music on Records from the 1890s to 1980s*. New York: Frederick Ungar, 1960.

B138   Rehramer, George. *The Macmillan Film Bibliography*. New York: Macmillan, 1982.

B139   *S.O.B.* film review. *Hollywood Reporter*, 6/22/81.

B140   *S.O.B.* film review. *Los Angeles Times*, 6/28/81.

B141   *S.O.B.* film review. *New Republic*, 6/18/81.

B142   *S.O.B.* film review. *Saturday Review*, 7/81.

B143   Schickel, Richard. *The Disney Version*. New York: Avon Books, 1974.
Includes information on the making of *Mary Poppins*.

B144   Schuster, Mel. *Motion Picture Performers: A Bible of Magazine and Periodical Articles* (1960-1969, plus 1970-74 supplement). Metuchen, NJ: Scarecrow Press, 1971 and 1974.

B145   "Second Annual American Comedy Awards, The." *TV Guide*, 5/28/88. Commentary on ABC-TV special, featuring Julie.

B146   "Second Annual American Comedy Awards, The." *Variety*, 5/14/88. Review of ABC-TV special, featuring Julie.

B147   Sennett, Ted. *Hollywood Musicals*. New York: Harry N. Abrams, Inc., 1968.

B148   Shipman, D. "The All-Conquering Governess." *Films and Filming*, 8/66.

B149   Shipman, David. *The Great Movie Stars: The International Years*. New York: Hill and Wang, 1972 and 1980.

B150   Shulman, Arthur and Roger Youman. *How Sweet it Was*. New York: Shorecrest, Inc., 1966.
Photos and brief data on Julie's early television appearances in the U.S.

B151   Shulman, Arthur and Roger Youman. *The Television Years*. New York: Popular Library, 1973.
Re-edited paperback version of the Shulman/Youman book, *How Sweet it Was* (see previous entry). Photos and brief data on Julie's early television appearances in the U.S.

B152   Smith, Gene. "Someday it Will All Be Just Wonderful." *Saturday Evening Post*, 1/29/66.

B153   "Sound of Christmas, The." *People*, 12/21/87.
Review of Julie's December 1987 ABC-TV special.

B154   *Sound of Music* videocassette film review. *Parent's*, 11/85.

B155   "Star Brights." *Redbook*, 11/86.
Interview with Julie's stepdaughter, Jennifer Edwards.

B156   Stern, Lee Edward. *The Movie Musical*. New York: Pyramid Communications, 1974.

B157   Stevenson, Isabelle. *The Tony Award*. New York: Crown Publishers, 1987.
Includes list of nominations and wins for Julie's three Broadway shows.

B158   Syse, Glenda. "Thoroughly Modern Julie Andrews." *Chicago Sun-Times*, 1/24/88.
General interview with Julie on the occasion of her 1987-1988 concert tour.

B159   Taylor, John Russell and Arthur Jackson. *The Hollywood Musical*. New York: McGraw Hill, 1971.

B160   Terrace, Vincent. *Encyclopedia of TV Series, Pilots, and Specials, 1973-1984*. New York: New York Zoetrope, 1985.

B161 Terrace, Vincent. *Television 1970-1980*. San Diego, CA: A. S. Barnes, 1981.

B162 *That's Life!* film review. *California*, 10/6/86.

B163 *That's Life!* film review. *Los Angeles*, 9/86.

B164 *That's Life!* film review. *MacLean's*, 10/6/86.

B165 *That's Life!* film review. *Newsweek*, 10/6/86.

B166 *That's Life!* film review. *Time*, 9/29/86.

B167 *That's Life!* film review. *Wall Street Journal*, 10/9/86.

B168 *That's Life!* videocassette review. *New York Times*, 11/15/87.

B169 *Theatre World Annual (London) 1953-54*. New York: Macmillan, 1954.
Includes details on Julie's London stage appearance in *Cinderella*.

B170 *Theatre World Annual (London) June 1, 1957- May 31, 1958*. New York: Macmillan, 1958.
Includes details on Julie's London stage appearance in *My Fair Lady*.

B171 Thomas, Tony and Aubrey Solomon. *The Films of 20th Century-Fox*. Secaucus, NJ: Citadel Press, 1979 and 1985.
Panoramic history of 20th Century-Fox films includes brief discussions of *The Sound of Music* and *Star!*

B172 Thompson, Howard. "Julie Andrews Starts Film Here." *New York Times*, 5/18/67.
Filming of *Star!* at Cort Theatre in New York.

B173 Thomson, David. *A Biographical Dictionary of Films*. New York: William Morrow & Co., 1976.

B174 Turner, A. K. "Julie Edwards (Andrews)." *Publishers Weekly*, 7/22/74.
Interview with Julie on the occasion of her second children's book (*The Last of the Really Great Whangdoodles*) being released.

B175 *Variety International Show Business Reference 1983*. New York and London: Garland Publishing, 1983.

B176 Viorst, Judith. Review of Julie's book *The Last of the Really Great Whangdoodles. New York Times*, 11/3/74.

B177 *Variety*. New York: Variety, Inc., 1/11/89.
Cumulative film rental receipts to date for all of Julie's films that accrued more than $4 million in U. S. and Canada.

B178 Vinson, John. *International Directory of Films and Filmmakers, Vol. III, Actors and Actresses*. Chicago and London: St. James Press, 1986.
Includes biographical data on Julie.

B179 Warner, Alan. *Who Sang What on the Screen?* North Rhyde, Australia: Angus & Robertson, 1984.

B180 Wells, Ted. "My Daughter, Julie Andrews." *Good Housekeeping*, 3/68.

B181 Westbury Music fair concert review. *New York Times*, 12/20/87.

B182 Whitney, Dwight. "Miss Andrews' Appointment with Television." *TV Guide*, 12/9/72.
 Detailed cover story discusses the factors leading up to Julie's decision to come to series TV and the subsequent preparations.

B183 Wiley, Mason and Damien Bona. *Inside Oscar: The Unofficial History of the Academy Awards*. New York: Ballantine Books, 1986.
 Behind-the-scenes details at each Oscar ceremony, including the four attended by Julie.

B184 Wilkins, B. "Soothing Blake Edwards and Raising Babies Result in a Thoroughly Joyous Julie." *People*, 3/77.

B185 Windeler, Robert. *Julie Andrews, A Biography*. New York: St. Martin's Press, 1970 and 1983
 Most comprehensive biography on Julie Andrews to date. A basically balanced portrait -- neither all praising nor all condemning. The 1983 edition was updated extensively, including several useful appendices and updated information throughout the book.

Appendix A
Awards and Nominations

Mary Poppins (1964)

Win for Julie:
- ■ Best Actress

Other Wins for the film:
- ■ Score: Richard M. Sherman and Robert B. Sherman
- ■ Song: "Chim-Chim-Cheree" (Shermans)
- ■ Editing: Cotton Warburton
- ■ Visual Effects: Peter Ellenshaw

Other Nominations
- ■ Best Picture
- ■ Director: Robert Stevenson
- ■ Screenplay: Bill Walsh and Don DeGradi
- ■ Cinematography (Color): Edward Colman
- ■ Sound: Disney Studio Sound Department
- ■ Art Direction/Set Decoration (Color): Carroll Clark, William H. Tuntke, Emile Karl, Hal Gausman
- ■ Costumes (Color): Tony Walton
- ■ Scoring: Irwin Kostal

The Americanization of Emily (1964)

Nominations :
- ■ Cinematography (Black-and-white): Philip H. Lathrop
- ■ Art Direction/Set Decoration (Black-and-white): George W.Davis, Hans Peters, Elliot Scott, Henry Grace, Robert H. Benton

The Sound of Music (1965)

Nomination for Julie
■   Best Actress

Wins for the film
■   Best Picture
■   Director: Robert Wise
■   Sound: Fox Sound Department
■   Score: Irwin Kostal
■   Editing: William Reynolds

Other Nominations
■   Supporting Actress: Peggy Wood
■   Cinematography (Color): Ted McCord
■   Art Direction/Set Decoration (Color): Boris Leven, Walter M. Scott, Ruby Levitt)
■   Costumes: Dorothy Jeakins

Hawaii (1966)

Nominations
■   Supporting Actress: Jocelyn LeGarde
■   Score: Elmer Bernstein
■   Song ("My Wishing Doll"): Music by Bernstein; lyrics by Mack David
■   Sound: Samuel Goldwyn Studio Sound Department
■   Costumes (Color): Dorothy Jeakins
■   Cinematography (Color): Russell Harlan

Thoroughly Modern Millie (1967)

Win for the film
■   Original Music Score: Elmer Bernstein

Other Nominations
■   Supporting Actress: Carol Channing
■   Art Direction/Set Decoration: Alexander Golitzen, George C. Webb, Howard Bristol
■   Costume Design: Jean Louis
■   Title Song: Sammy Cahn, Jimmy Van Heusen
■   Scoring: Andre Previn, Joseph Gershenson

Star! (1968)

Nominations
■   Supporting Actor: Daniel Massey
■   Cinematography: Ernest Laszlo
■   Art Direction/Set Decoration: Boris Leven, Walter M. Scott, Howard Bristol
■   Costume Design: Donald Brooks
■   Sound: Fox Sound Department
■   Title Song: Sammy Cahn, Jimmy Van Heusen
■   Scoring: Lennie Hayton

Darling Lili (1970)

Nominations :
- Costume Design: Donald Brooks and Jack Bear
- Song ("Whistling Away the Dark"): Music: Henry Mancini; lyrics: Johnny Mercer
- Original Song Score: Mancini/Mercer

10 (1979)

Nominations
- Score: Henry Mancini
- Song ("It's Easy to Say"): Music by Mancini; lyrics by Robert Wells)

Victor/Victoria (1982)

Nomination for Julie
- Best Actress

Other Nominations
- Supporting Actress: Lesley Ann Warren
- Supporting Actor: Robert Preston
- Screenplay: Blake Edwards
- Art Direction/Set Decoration: Roger Maus, Tim Hutchinson, William C. Smith, Harry Cordwell
- Original Score: Leslie Bricusse and Henry Mancini
- Costumes: Patricia Norris

That's Life! (1986)

Nomination
- Song ("Life in a Looking Glass"): Music by Henry Mancini; lyrics by Leslie Bricusse

---

Tonys

My Fair Lady (1957 awards; 1956 opening)

Nomination for Julie
- Best Actress in a Musical

Wins
- Best Musical
- Actor in a Musical: Rex Harrison
- Director: Moss Hart
- Author of a Musical: Alan Jay Lerner
- Producer: Herman Levin
- Scenic Designer: Oliver Smith
- Costume Designer: Cecil Beaton

Nominations
- ■ Composer: Frederick Loewe
- ■ Actor (Supporting or Featured) in a Musical: Stanley Holloway
- ■ Actor (Supporting or Featured) in a Musical: Robert Coote
- ■ Conductor and Musical Director: Franz Allers
- ■ Choreography: Hanya Holm

Camelot (1961 awards; 1960 opening)

Nomination for Julie
- ■ Best Actress in a Musical

Wins
- ■ Actor in a Musical: Richard Burton
- ■ Conductor and Musical Director: Franz Allers
- ■ Scenic Designer: Oliver Smith
- ■ Costume Designer: Adrian and Tony Duquette

Emmys

Cinderella (CBS; 1957)

Nomination for Julie
- ■ Best Actress in a Single Performance -- Lead or Support

Other Nominations
- ■ Live Camera Work
- ■ Music Contribution: Richard Rodgers

Julie and Carol at Carnegie Hall (1962-63)

Wins
- ■ Program Achievement (Music)
- ■ Performer in a Variety or Musical Program or Series: Carol Burnett (for this show and for *Carol and Company*)

The Andy Williams Show (1964/65)

Nomination for Julie
- ■ Individual Achievements in Entertainment (Actors and Performers)

The Julie Andrews Show (1965/66)

Win
- ■ Director of Variety or Music Program: Alan Handley

Nominations
- ■ Writing of Variety Program: Bill Persky, Sam Denoff
- ■ Individual Achievement in Conducting: Irwin Kostal
- ■ Individual Achievement in Electronic Production -- Special Electronic Effects: Milt Altman

Julie and Carol at Lincoln Center (1971-72)

Nominations
- Outstanding Single Program (Variety or Musical):
  Joe Hamilton, Producer
- Director: David P. Powers
- Writer (Comedy, Variety, or Music): Bob Ellison, Marty Farrell, Ken and Mitzi Welch

The Julie Andrews Hour (1972-73)

Wins
- Variety/Musical Series: Nick Vanoff and William O. Harbach, Producers and Julie Andrews, Star
- Director: Bill Davis
- Art Direction/Scenic Design (Variety or Music): Brian Bartholomew and Karen S. Walker
- Lighting Direction (Electronic TV): Track Krane
- Costume Design: Jack Bear
- Video Tape Editing: Nick Giordano and Arthur Schneider
- Technical Direction and Electronic Camerawork: Ernie Buttleman (Technical Director); Robert A. Kemp, James Angel, James Balden, Dave Hilmer (Cameramen)

Nominations
- New Series
- Choreography: Tony Charmoli
- Writing (Variety or Music): Bob Ellison, Hal Goodman, Larry Klein, Jay Burton, George Bloom, Lila Garrett, John Aylesworth, and Frank Peppiatt

Julie Andrews' Invitation to the Dance with Rudolph Nuryev (The CBS Festival of Lively Arts For Young People; 1980/81)

Win
- Outstanding Children's Informational/Instructional Special: Jack Wohl and Bernard Rothman, Producers

Nomination for Julie
- Individual Achievement in Children's Programming (Performers)

The Sound of Christmas (1987)

Wins
- Music Direction: Ian Fraser, Chris Boardman, Alexander Courage, Angela Morley)
- Music and Lyrics: Larry Grossman, Buz Cohan
- Editing: Andy Zall, Mark West, Bob Jenkis
- Lighting Direction: John Rook
- Technical Direction: Mike Spencer, David Barber, Bob Keys, Ron Sheldon, Gunter Degn

Grammys

Camelot original cast album (1960)

Nomination
- Show Album Original Cast

Mary Poppins film soundtrack(1964)

Winner
- Children's Recording
- Original Score of a Motion Picture or Television Show

The Sound of Music film soundtrack(1965)

Nomination
- Album of the Year

My Fair Lady (1977)

Hall of Fame Winner (Original Broadway cast recording from 1956)

Victor/Victoria (1982)

Nomination
- Original Score of a Motion Picture or Television Special

Other Awards and Nominations

- *Golden Globe*   Best Actress in a Comedy or Musical
  (*Mary Poppins*), 2/9/65 (Win)

  Best Actress in a Comedy or Musical
  The Sound of Music), 2/66 (Win)

  Best Actress in a Comedy or Musical
  (*Victor/Victoria*), 1/83 (Win)

  Best Actress in a Comedy or Musical
  (*That's Life!*), 1/87 (Nomination)

  Best Actress in a Drama
  (*Duet For One*), 1/87 (Nomination)

  Female World Film Favorite of 1966

  Female World Film Favorite of 1967

- Harvard University's Hasty Pudding Award (2/17/83)

- People's Choice Award for Film Acting (1983)
- Roses of Montreaux   *Julie and Carol at Carnegie Hall* (1962)

  The Julie Andrews Hour (1973)

  The Sound of Christmas (1988) (Nomination)
- British Academy Award 1964: Most Promising Newcomer (*Mary Poppins*)

Appendix B
Roles Julie (Almost) Played

Julie's Voice Only

●   Hardly the high point of Julie's career, *The Singing Princess* was an animated children's movie released in the U.S. in 1967. The movie, an Arabian Nights fairy tale, was originally produced in Italy in 1949 under the title *La Rosa di Bagdad.*
    It was redubbed in English in 1952. A very young Julie, in the role of Princess Zeila, sang "Song for the Bee," "Sunset Prayer," and "The Flower Song."
    Released by Larry Joachim Productions at the peak of Julie's popularity, the English-dubbed version was billed to star "the magic voice of Julie Andrews." The film was offered in 50 metropolitan areas as a weekend kiddie matinee. The *New York Times* (11/13/67) called it "feeble entertainment" and commented further: "Those pristine, silvery tones sounded like her [Julie] on Saturday, but in the diction department, she could have learned a thing or two from the Andrews Sisters."
    The 66-minute film is available on VHS cassette from Good Times Video.

●   *The Pink Panther Strikes Again*, a 1976 Peter Sellers (Inspector Clouseau) film by Julie's husband Blake Edwards, might be thought of as a precursor to Edwards' and Julie's 1982 film *Victor/Victoria*. In *Panther*, Julie's singing voice (in low register) is dubbed in as the voice of a performing female impersonator in a gay bar scene in the comedy. The song is called "Until You Love Me." (She is billed on the United Artists film soundtrack as *Ainsley Jarvis*.) In *Victor/Victoria*, Julie played a female singer who pretends to be a male female impersonator.
    An interesting sidelight: Blake Edwards had planned to team Julie with Peter Sellers in *Victor/Victoria*, but when Sellers died, the role was taken by Robert Preston.

Cutting Room Floor

    Julie *almost* had a film credit in Blake Edwards' 1975 Inspector Clouseau comedy *The Return of the Pink Panther*. She filmed a cameo sequence as a chambermaid, but the sequence was edited out of the release print. Edwards hoped to use the sequence in *The Trail of the Pink Panther* (1982), the *Panther* film he completed after Peter Sellers' death -- mostly consisting of outtakes from previous *Panther* films. However, the footage could not be found at the time.

Unconfirmed reports indicate that a brief part of this footage *did* appear in one of the *Panther* films. If so, it must be extremely fleeting, because it is impossible to spot.

Roles Julie Wasn't Offered

- *The Boy Friend* film (1971; Twiggy played Julie's stage role of Polly).

- The *My Fair Lady* film (1964; Audrey Hepburn played Julie's stage role of Eliza Doolitte).

- The *Camelot* film (1967; Vanessa Redgrave played Julie's stage role of Guenevere).

- Title roles in the *Mame* (1974) and *Hello, Dolly!* (1969) films (she had been announced as being among the actresses under consideration).

- Belinda in *The Public Eye* (1972), the Ross Hunter film of Peter Shaffer's one-act stage comedy. Originally discussed as a Mike Nichols film project to star Julie, and ultimately made by Ross Hunter starring Mia Farrow and Topol.

- The role of Anna opposite Yul Brynner in a revival of *The King and I*. Brynner did several revivals, but none with Julie as costar (although the producers considered her).

Projects Discussed for Julie (Never Made)

- *Mary Poppins II* for Disney. (With the success of Disney's live action/animation film, *Who Framed Roger Rabbit?*, perhaps *Poppins* would fly now.)

- *The Sound of Music II* for 20th-Century Fox. (Who could fill the shoes of Rodgers and Hammerstein?)

- MGM musicals including *Say It With Music* and *She Loves Me* (shelved by the studio in the 70's when musicals came to be regarded as boxoffice poison).

- *Jazz Babies*, costarring Carol Channing for Ross Hunter, as a followup to *Thoroughly Modern Millie*.

- Stage musical based on the film *Victor/Victoria*.

- Stage revivals of *My Fair Lady* and *Camelot* starring Julie.

- Blake Edwards film version of her children's book *The Last of the Really Great Whangdoodles*.

- The wife in the proposed film version of the Tom Jones/Harvey Schmitt musical *I Do! I Do!*, which starred Robert Preston and Mary Martin onstage.

Roles Julie Turned Down

- A small part in *The Devil's Disciple*, starring Kirk Douglas and Burt Lancaster.

- Velvet in *International Velvet*, the sequel to Elizabeth Taylor's classic, *National Velvet*. *International Velvet* was made in 1978 with Tatum O'Neal, Christopher Plummer, and Nanette Newman as Velvet.

- Tatum O'Neal's mother in the tearjerker *Six Weeks*, eventually made in 1982 with Mary Tyler Moore in the role offered to Julie and Katherine Healey in the role planned for O'Neal. Dudley Moore costarred.

- The apprentice witch in Disney's *Bedknobs and Broomsticks* (1971), which aspired to be another *Mary Poppins*, but missed by a long shot. Angela Lansbury took the part. Smart move, Julie.

- Mickey Rooney's daughter in *Pete's Dragon* (1977), yet another Disney attempt to out-Poppins *Poppins*. Helen Reddy took the sugar-and-spice role. Another smart move, Julie.

- The Barbara Harris stage role in *The Apple Tree*, the Jerry Bock/Sheldon Harnick Broadway musical.

Projects Julie Might Do (at this writing)

- Blake Edwards' sequel to *10*

- Another untitled film project planned by Blake Edwards

- Gershwin/Weill's *Lady in the Dark* on stage in England and/or the U.S.

- A new Andrews/Carol Burnett television special

- A TV special called *The Sound of Children*

- A children's book, *Babe*

Appendix C
Julie's Children's Books

MANDY
(New York: Harper & Row, 1971)

The first book to be authored by Julie (under her married name, Julie Edwards) was this fanciful tale about a lonely orphan who lives in an abandoned cottage.

Publishers' Weekly (12/13/71) said of the effort, "leaves much to be desired...sketchy plot...Characterization is not developed...Sugar-coated and not very substantial."

Time magazine (12/27/71) noted, "Though _Mandy_ is selling like _The Whole Earth Catalogue_, it mainly proves that Julie Andrews has fondly read _The Secret Garden_ and deserves every success as a singer and film actress."

THE LAST OF THE REALLY GREAT WHANGDOODLES
(New York: Harper & Row, 1974)

Julie's second book was a fantasy adventure about a professor who takes a group of children on a journey to find a magic land.

Does it sound like _The Wizard of Oz? Publisher's Weekly_ (5/27/74) thought so, but did not perceive that as a detriment. In fact, the review commented that youngsters would be "irresistibly reminded of Oz, not only because of the odd creatures but because of the sunny, colorful _feel_ of the place and the simply sketched but appealing humans who visit it. It's a book many children are going to love, and it would make a fine semi-animated movie." (Blake Edwards began planning such a film, but it was never made.)

The _New York Times_ (11/3/74) was not so enthusiastic in its appraisal: "Unfortunately, Julie (Andrews) Edwards is more committed to improving her young readers than she is in entertaining them, and her book is sunk by an overload of virtue."

Subject Index

The following notes about the organization of the book should be helpful in your understanding of how to use the index.

The book begins with an introductory preface, followed by a brief biography and chronology, which serve to summarize the major events of Julie's life.

The next four chapters cover her major career achievements in detail, including Filmography, Stage Appearances (including theatre, concerts, and live personal appearances), Television Appearances, and Discography. All of the individual entries in each of these four sections correspond to a particular career achievement and are numbered consecutively for convenient use of the subject index and for cross referencing within the chapters. Career events in each section are listed chronologically, then numbered consecutively. Filmography entries begin with **F01**...etc., Stage Appearances with **S01**...etc., Television Appearances with **T01**...etc., and Discography entries with **D01**...etc.

For example, her first film *Mary Poppins* is assigned number **F01**, her eighteenth film, *Duet For One*, number **F18**. If you are reading about *Mary Poppins* in the Filmography section and you want to know what songs were included in the film, the *Poppins* synopsis tells you to turn to Discography entry number **D15**, where the *Mary Poppins* film soundtrack is detailed. The Television Appearances and Stage Appearances sections use the same method to refer to soundtracks and cast albums, listing musical numbers for the television shows and stage productions in the Discography section only.

Following the four career event chapters is a bibliography (with entries numbered **B01**,...etc.), listing more than 150 reference sources for more information on Julie, including books, and magazine and newspaper articles.

The appendices include a list of various show business awards that Julie has won or received nominations for, including Oscars, Tonys, Emmys, Grammys, Golden Globes, and others (Appendix A), a list of theatre and film projects Julie *almost* performed in (Appendix B), and descriptions of the two children's books that Julie has written (Appendix C).

The Subject Index makes use of both page numbers and section entry numbers (such as **F01, S01, T01, D01**) for reference. For each index entry, I have used whichever method appeared to be the quickest way for the reader to locate a particular topic. In some cases (usually for shorter entries), the section entry numbers were better. In other cases, the page numbers seemed more helpful.

The index entries follow.

About the Author

LES SPINDLE is Senior Editor at EESof in Westlake Village, California, where he writes and edits user manuals for computer software. He is former editor of *Interface Age* and *Computing for Business*, and has authored hundreds of magazine and newspaper articles about entertainment and show business. Spindle also served for several years as Producer/Director of the Tiffany Playhouse in Albuquerque, New Mexico.